T0209754

Living TESTIMONIES

STORIES OF GOD'S FAITHFULNESS

A.J. GARY

WESTBOW
PRESS®
A DIVISION OF THOMAS NELSON
& ZONDERVAN

WestBow Press books may be ordered through booksellers or by contacting:

WestBow Press
A Division of Thomas Nelson & Zondervan
1663 Liberty Drive
Bloomington, IN 47403
www.westbowpress.com
1 (866) 928-1240

ISBN: 978-1-9736-8171-7 (sc)
ISBN: 978-1-9736-8173-1 (hc)
ISBN: 978-1-9736-8172-4 (e)

Library of Congress Control Number: 2019920162

Print information available on the last page.

WestBow Press rev. date: 12/20/2019

DEDICATION

This book is affectionately dedicated to my friend,
my helper, my Lord and the Savior of my soul,
Jesus.
May He receive all the glory and honor!

ACKNOWLEDGEMENTS

This book would not be in print without the support of my husband. Thank you for putting up with me all these years. I'm grateful to God for blessing me with the perfect counterpart. You are the love of my life!

To Christina and Nichole,
My girls.
Your talents, your beautiful spirits and your dedication to the Lord, bring the utmost joy to my heart. You are precious!

To Andrew and Joshua,
My boys.
For your technical skills, your honest input and your patience with a mom who sometimes doesn't finish her sentences, thank you. You are gems!

To Sharon and Laura,
Thank you for applying your gifts of grammar and spelling to this work. You are treasured. *The readers thank you, too!*

To all of those who contributed their God Stories,
You are sweet brothers and sisters in Christ and it is an honor to share your accounts of God's amazing work in your lives. Keep spreading the Good News!

PREFACE

Have you ever wondered what the world would be like if Jesus had not come? If you call Jesus Lord, then like me, the picture would be grim. Without the Savior's sacrifice, we would be living in a virtual nightmare.

Now consider where the world would be if the first Christians had never shared the Gospel message? If Jesus' sacrifice remained unknown, the world would be living in hopelessness.

Today the world drowns in sin. People everywhere live without hope. Yet, we have the Good News because someone told **us** about Jesus. So, the question is, "What are we doing with the Gospel?"

Jesus wants us to spread the news that He came to bring life. Eternal life! The greatest gift the world has ever known is in our hands. We shouldn't keep it to ourselves.

INTRODUCTION

The following pages are filled with testimonies and truths that will exhort and inspire you to a greater knowledge of God's faithfulness.

Like stones of remembrance, our God Stories can lift us up when we face tribulation. Each recollection of God's deliverance can motivate us in our spiritual walk. Additionally, by sharing these accounts of God's trustworthiness, others are built up in the faith.

This book is intended to highlight God's goodness. Some of these devotions are simple truths from God's word. Others are true stories about God's impact in the lives of His children.

May each testimony help to set your focus on the One who truly deserves all the praise and glory.

Be encouraged to share what God is doing in your life!

"Declare his glory among the nations, his marvelous deeds among all peoples."

Psalm 96:3 (NIV)

DIVINE DECLARATION

The story of Nebuchadnezzar's 2nd dream is found in the fourth chapter of Daniel and begins:

"Nebuchadnezzar the king, to all peoples, nations, and languages that dwell in all the earth: Peace be multiplied to you. I thought it good to declare the signs and wonders that the Most High God has worked for me. ... I, Nebuchadnezzar, was at rest in my house, and flourishing in my palace. I saw a dream which made me afraid, and the thoughts on my bed and the visions of my head troubled me." (Daniel 4:1-2, 4-5 NKJV)

He goes on to explain how Daniel interpreted his dream, how the dream came true and ultimately how God changed his life. The king's dream was a warning and a prophecy. Daniel knew that if Nebuchadnezzar didn't repent, the episode of madness foretold would take place.

Unfortunately, he did not repent but lifted himself in pride and after twelve months, he was struck with insanity. Driven to the fields like an animal, he lived for seven years in the wild.

Then in verse 34 we read,

"And at the end of the time I, Nebuchadnezzar, lifted my eyes to heaven, and my understanding returned to me; and I blessed the Most High and praised and honored Him who lives forever: For His dominion is an everlasting dominion, and His kingdom is from generation to generation." (Daniel 4:34 NKJV)

God did a mighty work in this Gentile king. But what I most want to point out is that Nebuchadnezzar shared his story! Note that it is written in the first person – *"I, Nebuchadnezzar..."*

Think about that. A powerful ruler, worshipper of the Babylonian god Bel, writing a chapter in the Hebrew Holy Scriptures about how the one true God changed his heart. Nebuchadnezzar recognized who God was and the impact was so great that he knew he had to share it.

This is what it's all about: sharing who God is so that He can be made known to others.

As this Gentile king candidly said, *"I thought it good to declare the signs and wonders that the Most High God has worked for me."* (Dan 4:2 NKJV) Indeed!

I hope this encourages you to share what God is doing in your life.

"But he was rebuked for his wrongdoing
by a donkey—an animal without
speech—who spoke with a human voice
and restrained the prophet's madness."

2 Peter 2:16 (NIV)

A SILLY SONG

It amazes me what God uses to accomplish His work, to encourage or exhort.

While at a hotel, on a women's retreat, my friends and I decided to write a song for a sister in the Lord who blessed us with one of her *legendary* cheesecakes. As a "Thank you" gesture, we rewrote the lyrics to several songs from *The Sound of Music.*

The verses comically expressed our weakness for cheesecake and our inability to share it; all to the tune of *"the hills are alive…", "how do you solve a problem like Maria,"* and *"I am sixteen, going on seventeen."* The final verse showed a willingness to distribute slices to our friends.

Our witty composition, sung in three-part harmony, turned out to be a hilarious medley that amused many of women that attended the retreat.

But God decided to use our silly songwriting to change a heart.

It happened while we were still in the process of writing the song. Late in the evening, sitting by the pool, the three of us practiced the verses softly. As our harmonies echoed quietly throughout the tiled room, several women meandered about.

One woman in particular had come to grab a snack from the refreshment table. She was upset that one of her roommates had eaten some goodies from a plate she had left in their room. What was especially irritating was that her piece of cheesecake was gone. It had been the last piece and she looked forward to enjoying it. Yet, when she returned to the room with her cup of coffee, the plate had been plundered.

With resentment in her heart, she surveyed the remaining desserts until her ears caught wind of the song. She had thought it was worship practice, but then the words became clear. It was a song about cheesecake and it ended with; *"Now I'm finally ready to slice it, and share my cheesecake with you."*

Needless to say, God had spoken to her heart. With a smile on her face, she confessed to our pastor's wife how God used a song to change her heart – even a silly song.

"But God, who is rich in mercy,…"

Ephesians 2:4a (NKJV)

BUT GOD

Tom was a prodigal. He walked away from God and started dating Judy. She was a free-spirited unbeliever who thought nothing of God. Being with her fulfilled Tom's desire to be as distant from God as possible. When he married her in his early twenties, Judy was pregnant and Tom's parents wondered how their son would ever return to Christ.

But God;

At 22, Judy discovered a lump in her throat. Doctors said the golf-ball size mass would have to be surgically removed before they could tell if it was cancerous. In addition, her vocal chords were at risk for damage.

Judy was scared. She was young, with a baby to care for, and now she faced an uncertain future. Would she lose her voice? Would she die? Her anxiety increased day-to-day. Though she concealed it, depression overwhelmed her.

One evening, Judy sat at her kitchen table with a friend at her left and Tom at her right. Their conversation turned to religion and her friend remarked, "Why do people even go to church?"

Tom's Christian upbringing triggered a clear-cut answer. "Christians want to know God, so they go to church to learn His Word." "It's not about religion," he continued, "It's about having a personal relationship with Jesus. He died on a cross for our sins, so we can spend eternity in heaven with Him."

As Tom continued sharing the Gospel message, Judy listened intently. These were words of life to her tormented soul, and every syllable quickened her heart.

"You simply need to accept Jesus," Tom's lips proclaimed, "It's not about what we have to offer; it's all about faith." This was truth and Judy knew it. She excused herself from the table, went into the bathroom and knelt down. She cried a desperate prayer to Jesus and when she stood up, she felt an enormous weight vanish.

The following day, her mother-in-law called. Judy asked her where to buy a Bible and find a good church. Her mother-in-law was thrilled at Judy's conversion and a few years later, Tom, too, came back to Christ.

Judy continues to walk closely with Jesus today, knowing He stepped in to redeem her through the words of a prodigal - God's plan of redemption for both of them.

"But God demonstrates his own love for us in this: While we were still sinners, Christ died for us."

Romans 5:8 (NIV)

THE WRONG QUESTION

The courtroom was tense. The prosecutor impatiently waited for the defendant to answer his question. "A simple 'yes' or 'no' will do," he ordered. The litigant fumbled for words, "I can't answer that." The lawyer irately demanded a response then looked to the judge.

"Please answer the question," the judge insisted. "Your honor, if I answer that question, I will incriminate myself," he tried to explain. "Then he must be guilty," shouted the prosecutor. The judge furrowed his brow, "You must answer."

Finally, the defendant asked, "Sir, before I answer, may I ask the prosecutor a question?" The lawyer was annoyed, but the judge conceded. "Mr. Prosecutor, I wish to ask you a simple yes or no question. Have you stopped beating your wife?"

Appalled, the lawyer lashed out, "I don't beat my wife. How dare you imply such a thing?" The defendant interjected,

"A simple 'yes' or 'no' will do." The judge smiled insightfully, "Will the prosecutor please rephrase the question."

The lawyer's question made allegations about the defendant, without giving room for defense. Asking the lawyer if he stopped beating his wife showed that the lawyer asked the wrong question. By answering either yes or no, the lawyer would have implicated that he had beaten his wife at some point.

Often, people tend to question God like that. They say, "If God is good, why did He let this happen?" Ultimately, He isn't just a "good" God, He is the definition of "good". Bad things don't happen because of God, bad things happen because of sin, our sin.

The fact that God allows bad things to happen doesn't make Him less good. In fact, in His goodness, He allows us to live (which is why there is evil in the first place) AND gives us a chance to enter into a relationship with Him. Otherwise, He could wipe us out in an instant and be righteous to do so, because *"There is no one righteous, not even one;"* (Romans 3:10 NIV)

The question shouldn't be "God, why do you let bad things happen to good people?" but, "God, why do you allow good things to happen to bad people?"

"Known to God from eternity are all His works."

Acts 15:18 (NKJV)

HE KNOWS!

Some people believe that God is not really in control; like He's sitting in the heavens as a spectator, trying to make the best of it. Others believe He made the earth and everything in it and let it alone. Nothing could be farther from the truth. *"Known to God from eternity"* (Acts 15:18 NKJV) – since the beginning of time itself, God has known *exactly* what He is going to do and how He is going to do it. Nothing can change His perfect will or timing.

Job is a great example. He was a righteous man who loved the Lord and sought to obey Him. Job was tested and tried beyond anything we can conceive. He lost his wealth and his children; his friends betrayed him; his wife told him to curse God and die, and finally, he lost his health. Through all this, Job remained faithful to the Lord. Job wrestled with the question "Why?" to which the Lord answered him in several chapters. Job responded: *"I know that You can do everything, and that **no purpose** of Yours can be withheld from You."* (Job 42:2 NKJV emphasis added)

Job came to the realization that *he* was not God and that God had the right to do *whatever* He wanted, *whenever* He wanted. He understood that God had perfect purpose, not only in allowing, but also in actually *doing* the things that caused difficulty in his life.

The book closes with an important statement. *"Then all his brothers, all his sisters, and all those who had been his acquaintances before, came to him and they consoled him and comforted him for all the adversity that **the Lord** had brought upon him."* (Job 42:11 NKJV emphasis added)

See, the Lord brought upon Job great difficulty in order to teach him a valuable lesson. *"I am the Alpha and the Omega, the first and the last, the beginning and the end."* (Revelation 22:13 NIV)

The Lord is in complete control, friends. You can know that He is good (Romans 8:28). You can be assured that His ways are perfect (Jeremiah 29:11). You can trust Him to be God (Exodus 3:14).

Whether you feel defeated or afflicted; shaken or downtrodden; anxious or afraid, believe this, ***"Known to God from eternity are all His works."*** (Acts 15:18 NKJV)

Contributing author: Nichole Smith

"Then I set my face toward the Lord God to
make request by prayer and supplications,
with fasting, sackcloth, and ashes."

Daniel 9:3 (NKJV)

PROMISES, PROPHECY AND PRAYER

Does God really care if we pray? After all, if He's in control, and He is going to do what He's planned, why bother?

As one of the greatest examples of Godliness in the Bible, Daniel answers that question.

Daniel had been a captive for more than 60 years when he read the prophecy in Jeremiah 25:1-11 and 29:1-10. God declared a period of 70 years for Israel's captivity. He didn't resign with the thought that whatever will be, will be. He got on his knees and prayed. Daniel 9 begins with this powerful and insightful prayer.

God gave a promise to Jeremiah who declared the prophecy and Daniel understood that he could share in the fulfillment of that word through prayer. He showed by his humble petition that God's promises encourage us to take part in His plan through prayer.

We can learn from Daniel's prayer, that God doesn't exclude us from His work – He calls us to share in it as partners to accomplish His heavenly agenda. We get to be a part of what God is doing, by calling on Him to fulfill His plan.

We must also note that Daniel prayed God's Word back to Him. How important it is to read God's Word! When we "hide" God's Word in our hearts, we can more readily pray with confidence, knowing that our prayers are in the will of God.

Spurgeon said, "Oh! It is grand praying when our mouth is full of God's word, for there is no word that can prevail with him like his own."

As Daniel prayed for the prompt fulfillment of Jeremiah's prophecy, we, too, can pray for the "hastening" of another prophecy. Jesus said, *"Watch therefore, for you do not know what hour your Lord is coming."* (Matthew 24:42 NKJV)

Our participation in prayer for Christ's return upholds Peter's plea that we should be, *"looking for and hastening the coming of the day of God."* (1 Peter 3:12 NKJV)

Considering the importance of prayer, we should eagerly lift up our petitions and praise to Him, not forgetting the last prayer in the Bible:

"Amen. Even so, come, Lord Jesus!" (Revelation 22:20 NKJV)

*"Consider one another in order to stir up
love and good works, not forsaking the
assembling of ourselves together,..."*

Hebrews 10:24-25 (NKJV)

SOME ASSEMBLY REQUIRED

Christians use many excuses for not going to church; "They're filled with hypocrites," "I listen to sermons online," "I don't need church, I study the Bible on my own," "It's boring, irrelevant, outdated, etc..."

So the question is, do Christians really need to go to church?

In the passage above, the writer of Hebrews is asking readers to consider each other in order to "excite or call into action" love and good works. This happens through assembling – the Greek word used here refers to a formal gathering of believers.

This passage certainly comes across as a command, if not in the least a binding request. Take into account the fact that the epistles in the New Testament were written to edify the body of believers; some addressed specifically to the local churches.

The context of these letters teaches how to get along with one another in the church, how to encourage the weak in the church, how to deal with unrepentant sinners in the church and how to use our gifts in the church. These would not be applicable if we were not part of a church.

Church attendance is not necessary for salvation, but like baptism and the breaking of bread in communion, it is an essential part of our Christian walk.

Consider 1 Corinthians 12:27, *"Now you are the body of Christ, and members individually,"* (NKJV) The fact that we are part of the body of Christ shows us that it's more than us as individuals. Just as a body needs its parts to function properly, so too, the church needs its members. Read 1 Corinthians 12:14–20 to understand the importance of the different "body parts".

Imagine a trip through the amputee ward of a hospital and you'll understand the necessity of each part. A person missing an arm or leg will not function in the same capacity as one who is physically whole.

God is a God of relationship. He instilled in us a need for one another. We were designed for fellowship, both to give of our gifts for the edification of others and to receive from others for our spiritual growth.

Following this instruction, let's be active body parts!

*"Look at the birds of the air, for they
neither sow nor reap nor gather into barns;
yet your heavenly Father feeds them. Are
you not of more value than they?"*

Matthew 6:26 (NKJV)

HIS EYE IS ON ...

At the end of a day of yardwork, my husband was trimming the bushes. As he worked on the last shrub, the battery operated hedge trimmer died. Exhausted from the day's work, he decided to leave the last crop of branches for another time. The bush stood obviously unfinished, with its leafy shoots protruding from the top.

Situated outside the front window, the misshaped shrub was unsightly. My husband knew he'd have to get to it soon. The next morning, as he looked out the window, the tuft of branches caught his eye. Then, the abrupt motion of a bird startled him. It had flown out of the bush. He drew closer to the window to get a look and there in the uncut sprigs lay a bird's nest with three tiny robins. The newly hatched babies bobbled with their open beaks in the air, waiting for momma bird to return with breakfast.

My husband and I were in awe. Every bush in the yard had been trimmed, including most of this one. All except for that one little spot.

Could it be that God was watching out for those tiny little creatures? Was it coincidence for the battery to die at precisely that point?

Jesus said, *"Are not two sparrows sold for a copper coin? And not one of them falls to the ground apart from your Father's will."* (Matthew 10:29 NKJV)

Our God is a loving Father who asks, *"Are you not of more value than they?"* (Matt 6:26 NKJV)

Jesus makes a point to tell us that our Father cares so much about us. He continues in Matthew 6:31-32, *"So do not worry, saying, 'What shall we eat?' or 'What shall we drink?' or 'What shall we wear?' For the pagans run after all these things, and your heavenly Father knows that you need them."* (NIV)

What worries you? Are there concerns that have you losing sleep? Do you fret about an impending need, wondering how you'll make it?

Remember Jesus' words, and like those little birds, expectantly wait on your gracious, heavenly Father to provide.

*"Behold, I stand at the door and knock.
If anyone hears My voice and opens
the door, I will come in to him and
dine with him, and he with Me."*

Revelation 3:20 (NKJV)

TEPID TENDANCIES

In this passage from the letter to the Laodicean church, Jesus was <u>not talking to unbelievers.</u> He was talking to "lukewarm" **Christians**! The Laodiceans had become so tepid in spirit that Jesus wanted to vomit them out of His mouth. Their self-sufficient attitude literally made Jesus sick!

Sometimes, living in comfort can cause us to feel "in control" and we can lose our dependency on God. We say, "I've got this, Lord, I don't need your help right now!" But, Jesus said, *"Without me, you can do NOTHING!"* (John 15:5b NKJV) So, if we think we can handle *anything* without Him, we disagree with the One we call Lord.

Additionally, when we believe that we have enough strength to handle, let's say, 80% of a situation, we will only lean on God for the 20% we lack. In essence, we ask God to "fill in the gap".

But His Word doesn't tell us to give it all we've got. Instead,

He says, *"My strength is made perfect in weakness."* (2 Corinthians 12:9 NKJV) God is looking for weaklings in the flesh, so He can become STRONG in them, and receive the glory for it. Why? Because, we're told that in our flesh, *"NOTHING good dwells."* (Romans 7:18 NKJV)

In addition to an easy life, we can also let the busyness of this world distract us, which causes us to set our time with God aside. This routine "cools" our passion for Him, because we can only stay warmed when we're close to the fire.

The wonderful news is that it's not too late. Jesus wants intimacy with us, but He will never force Himself on us. He's standing at the door, waiting for us to "open up" and let Him enter.

Jesus will ALWAYS give us victory in our battle to overcome complacency and fill us with a passion for Him *and* His Word. He only requires us to ask Him in all sincerity. That's what He meant when He said, *"If you ask anything in My name, I will do it."* (John 14:14 NKJV)

Ask Him to throw kindling on the embers of your heart.

*"The secret things belong to the Lord our
God, but those things which are revealed
belong to us and to our children forever,
that we may do all the words of this law"*

Deuteronomy 29:29 (NKJV)

IN THE KNOW

Homeschooling came with many rewarding moments and one precious memory concerns my son Andrew. At 4 years old, he was extremely inquisitive. One day he recited his numbers, counting up to 20. I continued with "Twenty-one, twenty-two, twenty-three…" wanting to extend his aptitude. He repeated after me and when we finished he asked, "Mommy, can you count all the way to the end?"

The question made me chuckle, yet it took a lengthy explanation to answer it in a way he could understand. Compared to adults, children's minds see things far more limited. Though we are all finite in nature, children tend to have much smaller boundaries intellectually. The younger they are, the smaller the world is in their eyes.

As adults, we comprehend the vastness of space, the complexity of nature and the intricacy of life. However, we realize that there is still so much we don't know. In fact, scientists say, the more they discover, the more they realize how much there still is to comprehend.

God created us with intelligence. Yet, our restricted minds are not capable of completely understanding Him as an infinite, immeasurable Being. *"Oh, the depth of the riches both of the wisdom and knowledge of God! How unsearchable are His judgments and His ways past finding out!"* (Romans 11:33 NKJV)

The incapacity to understand God fully should not hinder us from wanting to know Him intimately. In fact, it should inspire us to dig deeper into His word to gain a greater knowledge of Him.

Equally important is our acceptance that we will never know EVERYTHING about God. When we struggle through a trial and fight to know the reason why, we are often left frustrated. The fact is, some things are meant to be hidden from us. *"For My thoughts are not your thoughts, Nor are your ways My ways," says the Lord."* (Isaiah 55:8 NKJV)

Ultimately, when we dwell on what God has revealed to us, we will find peace. Know that God is *"compassionate and gracious, slow to anger, abounding in love."*(Psalm 103:8 NIV) and leave the unknown to Him.

"For thus says the Lord God of Israel:
'The bin of flour shall not be used up, nor
shall the jar of oil run dry, until the day
the Lord sends rain on the earth.'"

1 Kings 17:14 (NKJV)

FLAPJACKS ANYONE?

One morning, as I stood at the stove making pancakes, my son, Joshua, asked me a question. "How would you feel about having pancakes every day, for breakfast, lunch and dinner, for three years?"

I snickered, wondering what got my 22-year-old to think of such a thing. I answered, "I guess I'd get sick of them pretty quickly."

"But what if that was all there was to eat?" he responded with the question.

I admitted that I would be glad to have them to eat.

Then he asked me if I knew the true story to which he was referring. My eyebrows raised, my mind churned. *Who had to eat pancakes for three years?* I pondered while buttering the griddle for another batch.

Josh smiled. I hoped for a hint. He mentioned it was in the

Bible. I confessed the story didn't come to mind. Finally, he mentioned the widow and Elijah. "Of course!" I blurted out. They ate cakes made of flour and oil – pancakes.

I thought about it a minute and replied that I hadn't considered how they ate nothing but pancakes for so long a time. Yet, I'm sure they were grateful to have food.

By obeying Elijah, the widow showed her faith in God's Word and her obedience was rewarded with a fresh supply of flour and oil each day. She put God's prophet first and God sustained her throughout the famine.

I think what is most interesting is that God didn't just supply a huge quantity of flour that would last throughout the famine. Instead, He provided a daily portion.

It's possible God was protecting her from others. The severity of the famine could prompt the locals who heard about her huge supply of food to ransack her home and maybe even kill her in the process.

Additionally, God may have provided in this way, so the widow would rely on her faith in His promise each day. She would have to trust God daily – and so should we.

Make a habit of thanking God **daily** for His provision.

"He is before all things, and in him all things hold together."

Colossians 1:17 (NIV)

ATOMIC GLUE

An amazing discovery came with the advent of electron microscopes. With the ability to see inside the atom, scientists learned that they are 98% space. Each atom contains a nucleus, protons and electrons, and though they are miniscule, they are not dense. Every atom is predominantly empty.

Another marvel that was uncovered is that the protons and electrons remain together, in spite of the fact that their polarity should cause them to repel each other. In fact, the atomic bomb was created when scientists figured out that causing certain atoms to split created an immense amount of energy – hence nuclear power.

Of all the findings, the most incredible observation is that the energy to *hold the atoms together* is far greater than that which comes from splitting them apart. If you've ever seen an image of a nuclear explosion, you can understand how incredibly powerful that must be.

It is the greatest source of energy that exists, and scientists still don't know its origin. But, in order to put a name to this phenomenon, they came up with the title "Atomic Glue".

When we consider the awesome power of the Almighty Creator, we understand that God truly does hold things together. In fact, God held together the nails driven into Jesus' hands and feet. The same power bonded the hammer that pounded them through His flesh.

As a believer, that truth compels me to love Him all the more.

The world doesn't understand that reality. Blind to the truth, they take creation and life itself, for granted. It's easier for scientists to label something they don't know with a term that usurps a Godhead.

The Bible has the answer that unbelieving scientists are looking for – "*He is before all things, and in him all things hold together.*" (Colossians 1:17 NIV)

"As every effect depends upon its cause, and cannot exist without it; so creation, which is an effect of the power and skill of the Creator, can only exist and be preserved by a continuance of that energy that first gave it being." (Adam Clarke's Commentary on the Bible, Adam Clarke, LL.D., F.S.A., (1715-1832) pg. 1512)

Knowing who upholds creation, we marvel at the wonderful works of our almighty God!

"Moreover He said to me: "Son of man, receive into your heart all My words that I speak to you, and hear with your ears."

Ezekiel 3:10 (NKJV)

FIRST THINGS FIRST

I remember having a discussion with an unbeliever who was going through some trials. As I shared about my own struggles, he listened intently. I didn't realize how animated I had become while explaining how God had showered me with peace and filled me with joy in spite of my difficulties. When I finished, he let out a big sigh and remarked, "Wow! You're really passionate about your faith."

I just smiled, hoping he understood the message – that God is real, God is sovereign and that God loves him. When we finished our conversation, he admitted that he had heard many people talk about their faith, but in me, he could *see* it.

After we parted ways, I became aware of the power that had surged within me as I talked about God. By this divine influence, my friend was so deeply impressed. Yet, it wasn't me, it was a natural outpouring of the Holy Spirit.

God shows us how we can be filled with His divine effectiveness in His words to Ezekiel.

Ezekiel was called by God to be a prophet to the rebellious Israel. Chapter 1 describes his call and his incredible vision of heavenly beings. In chapter 3, God sends him out with a message, but *first things first* – he had to "receive" and "hear" God's word.

God knew His message would not get through to His people, if His messenger didn't truly have it in his own heart. The word "receive" is the Hebrew word "lâqach" which can be translated "accept" or "seize". Ezekiel needed to seize God's word and accept it fully.

And, God wanted him to "hear" it; "shâma" which means "hearing intelligently" and carries with it the idea of "perception, obedience, and proclamation".

Once Ezekiel fully accepted and perceived God's Word, he would be moved to obey and proclaim it to others.

Likewise, God calls us to be His witnesses. We too, need to seize every nugget of God's Word and let it effusively sink into our hearts. When we do, it will move us to understanding and obedience. Then we will be effective messengers for the kingdom.

*"For great is your love toward me; you
have delivered me from the depths, from
the realm of the dead. But you, Lord, are
a compassionate and gracious God, slow to
anger, abounding in love and faithfulness."*

Psalm 86:13,15 (NIV)

DELIVERED FROM DEATH

After months of dealing with a heart arrhythmia, I went in for a surgical procedure to correct it. The marginally invasive technique sends a catheter into the heart through an artery. An electrode then cauterizes the nerves that are "misfiring", causing the arrhythmia.

After hours on the operating table for which I was fully awake, my cardiologist informed me that he was calling it off. He explained that the most prominent nerve that needed targeting was near the center wall of the heart and presented a greater risk. It increased my chances of having a heart attack and he felt that it would be too risky to go ahead.

I assured him that I was okay with his decision and that God had other plans, but inside I was acutely disappointed. As

I got ready to go home, I noticed that a friend had texted me Psalm 86:13,15. In my discouragement, I read it superficially.

In an effort to cheer me, my husband took me to the beach for a picnic. The beautiful day lightened my attitude. When we got home, I looked again at the text from my friend. Her passage was from The Message. The words in verse 13- ***"You snatched me from the brink of disaster!"*** (Psalm 86:13 MSG) astonished me.

I wondered why she sent me this particular verse. I personally would not have forwarded it to someone going in for surgery. When I asked her, she explained that the passage was on her daily Scripture calendar and she felt God prompting her to send it to me. She resisted because she too, thought it was inappropriate. However, the Holy Spirit kept persuading and she sent it, not knowing the procedure had been called off.

Had I read it more carefully the first time, maybe I wouldn't have seen the cancelled surgery as a failure. I don't know what peril may have befallen me, but I do know that God's plan never fails.

Remarkably, months later, I noticed that my arrhythmia had virtually disappeared! God intended to heal me all along!

"He taught His disciples and said to them,
"The Son of Man is being betrayed into
the hands of men, and they will kill Him.
And after He is killed, He will rise the
third day." But they did not understand
this saying, and were afraid to ask Him."

Mark 9:31-32 (NKJV)

SOMETHING'S MISSING

In all four Gospels, Jesus predicts His death, yet the disciples never seemed to get it.

For three years, the disciples had seen Jesus' power through miracles and His authority over the religious leaders. However, they missed something. Their shortsightedness kept them from seeing the suffering Messiah.

It reminds me of the time I taught my young daughter how to clean the kitchen table after supper. She watched closely as I used the washcloth to gather all the crumbs together. Then, carefully I pushed the pile off the table into my hand.

The next day, after breakfast, she volunteered to clean up and I watched her meticulously gather the scraps of food into a little mound at the table's edge. Then, with great enthusiasm, she dragged the heap of crumbs *onto the **floor**.*

I was dumbfounded. "What are you doing?" I asked, mustering my composure. She looked at me, completely innocent. "It's just the way you showed me."

When I recalled my "lesson" the night before, I realized my daughter didn't see my left hand catching the crumbs. Her short stature only allowed her to observe me pushing the crumbs off the table. After a good laugh at the mishap, I showed her the "right way" to do the job.

She wasn't being disobedient or lazy when she dumped the scraps on the floor, she simply didn't understand the whole lesson.

There are times in life, that we miss God's instructions. We may see most of what He asks of us, but miss an imperative piece of the message. This lapse is usually due to our shortsightedness. Our spiritual immaturity masks our perception.

However, God is always aware of our shortcomings. He knows what we miss and is ready to repeat the instruction.

When we fail to grasp His divine lesson, are we willing to take the test again? If so, we'll be blessed. *"Whoever gives heed to instruction prospers, and blessed is the one who trusts in the Lord."* (Proverbs 16:20 NIV)

*"When Jesus heard it, He marveled, and
said to those who followed, "Assuredly,
I say to you, I have not found such
great faith, not even in Israel!"*

Matthew 8:10 (NKJV)

AMAZING FAITH

Recently I watched a documentary on several amazing cathedrals. I watched with fascination at the incredible engineering in these magnificent structures. The intricately sculpted carvings, painstakingly detailed mosaics and vibrantly colored stained glass windows were the works of some very talented architects and artists.

With the ability to see the wonders of the world through the technology of the internet, it's easy to find things that astound us. We can watch the feats of human strength and stamina, peruse the creations of masterful builders, artists and composers, and investigate the mysteries of nature - all leaving us greatly impressed.

In the New Testament, the Greek word thaumazō ("to marvel") is found numerous times. In the Gospels, we can read many instances of people who "marveled". Joseph and Mary marveled (Luke 2:33), Jesus' disciples marveled (Matt 8:27), the multitudes marveled (Matt 9:33 and others), the Pharisees marveled (Matt 22:22), Pilate marveled (Mark 15:5).

In each of these instances, Jesus is the subject of that amazement. The prophecies spoken of Him, His power over creation, His miraculous healings, His authority and wisdom and His humility, inspired awe.

It's interesting that only one thing seemed to amaze Jesus. There are only two mentions of Jesus marveling, and both times, He marveled at faith.

Both Matthew and Luke recount the story of Jesus visit to Capernaum, where a centurion pleads with Jesus to heal his servant. In his appeal, the Gentile commander shows great faith by accepting Jesus word. *"Lord, I am not worthy that You should come under my roof. But only speak a word, and my servant will be healed."*(Matthew 8:8 NKJV) This faith amazed Jesus.

In contrast, Mark 6:6 describes Jesus visit to His hometown. After teaching in the synagogue, many were offended by Him. Jesus *"marveled because of their unbelief,"* (NKJV) showing amazement at their "lack of faith".

Faith amazed Jesus when He found it in an unlikely candidate and equally amazed Him when He found it *missing* in those who should have had it.

May the power of the Holy Spirit help us stand in a faith that impresses our Lord!

*"The Lord watches over you— the Lord is
your shade at your right hand; the sun will not
harm you by day, nor the moon by night."*

Psalm 121:5-6 (NIV)

GOD'S BIG SHADOW

It was a bright summer day as Elissa stood with her young daughter in the mall parking lot. They were waiting for her friend to pick them up.

As the blazing sun beat down on them, her little one murmured, "I'm so hot, Mommy!"

Elissa was also hot, but how could she help young Olivia? There was no shelter to shield them from the sweltering sun. Then she looked down at her little girl and realized that she could cast a shadow big enough to shroud Olivia.

She positioned herself to eclipse the sun's scorching rays from her four-year-old's small frame. Moments later, Olivia began to relax and looked up at her mother. "Mommy, you're like a big cloud that makes it not be hot!"

That reminded Elissa of a Bible story.

"Did you know that God was a cloud?" she questioned. Olivia furrowed her brow and Elissa told her the story of God's people wandering in the desert. As the sun burned brightly in the sky, the Israelites were protected.

"God was a pillar of cloud by day," she explained, "shielding His children from the terrible heat." Olivia loved the story, and especially understood its meaning as she stood in the shade of her mother's shadow.

It was at that moment Elissa felt she heard God's quiet voice. She needed to step into His shade.

After months of difficulty, Elissa wanted to give up on God. Losing her job, her babysitter and a broken-down car was too much. She was an overwhelmed single mom and felt as if God didn't care. Now, waiting in this parking lot, God was showing her that His shadow was big enough for her.

Elissa surrendered her fears and instantly felt an unexplainable reassurance envelop her.

Sometimes the heat of a trial feels excessively hot, but God promises to protect us. He doesn't promise to extinguished the blaze, but assures us that He's there in our midst. God wants us to trust in Him, in spite of the heat. Like stepping into His shadow, our faith in Him will result in a refreshing peace.

"And God is able to make all grace abound toward you, that you, always having all sufficiency in all things, may have an abundance for every good work."

2 Corinthians 9:8 (NKJV)

FUTILE FORMULA

Remember Algebra? Plugging numbers into A, B and C to solve for X? Have you ever tried to place God in a formula? Calculating your Christian walk into something like - I sin, I disobey, I make the wrong choices = my life is bad and things go wrong. I obey, I act selflessly, I seek to please God = my life is good and things go the way I want them to.

However, this is a false notion. An infinite God can't be defined by a finite equation. This only gives us a picture of God based on how *we* think rather than on who He really is. Additionally, it causes us to live by works, thinking that if we keep doing the right things then we can find our worth.

Christian faith is founded on God's grace! Jesus' death on the cross for our sins should be our motivation to do the right things. *"We love Him because He first loved us."* (1 John 4:19 NKJV).

1 Corinthians 6:20 says, *"For you were bought at a price; therefore glorify God in your body and in your spirit, which are God's."* (NKJV) The truth is, we are not our own. Are you willing to be obedient to God, no matter the outcome? No matter the cost? Are you willing to say to Him, "Not my will but Yours"?

Don't put Him in a formula, rather, be willing to surrender everything. Give without expectation of anything in return. Love without reservation. Speak truth even if it means being rejected. Be obedient no matter the cost. Know that His grace is sufficient for you. Know that He will never leave you nor forsake you. Though you are hard pressed on every side, you are not crushed; perplexed, but not in despair; persecuted, but not forsaken; struck down, but not destroyed.

Praise the Lord that He never gives up on us. He proves Himself faithful time and time again and continues to work in our lives. May we daily make the choice to say, "Not my will, but Yours be done."

Contributing author: Nichole Smith

GOD'S CELESTIAL CALCULATOR

I remember teaching my kids the Metric system in homeschool. It especially interested me because I had only learned the Imperial method of measurement as a child. With an abundance of tools, we can measure length, weight, volume, light intensity, temperature, noise level, density, velocity, moisture, pressure, quantity, electrical conductivity, and the list goes on.

Some tools measure things on a miniscule scale, like the test that determines how many Leukemia cells are in my bloodstream. With this technology, my doctor has the capability of letting me know when I'm in remission. Other tools detect enormous dimensions, like the distance between stars.

Yet, in all my years, I have never heard of a tool to measure love. We may calculate the extent of someone's love by the things they do or the sincerity of their actions, but we make each estimation on an individual basis, resulting in an ambiguous factor.

When it comes to measuring God's love, however, an instrument exists that can quantify it. That instrument is the cross.

Like a compass rose that points in all directions, the cross leads us to look at the four dimensions of God's great love.

> *Left and Right*; where God's forgiveness casts our sins as far as the east is from the west (Psalm 103:12)

> *Down*; to the depths where Jesus, in death, descended into the heart of the earth to purchase redemption (Matt 12:40)

> *Up*; into heaven where Jesus has prepared a place for us in eternity. (John 14:2)

The verse says, "*..to know the love of Christ which passes knowledge;*" (Eph 3:19 NKJV) How can we **know** something that **exceeds knowledge**? Is Paul teasing us in this passage?

Consider that God's love is like the cosmos. Astronomers continually study and explore the universe – grasping the immensity of it, yet, knowing that they do not fully understand everything it contains. To them, it *passes knowledge.* God's love is similar. Its extent is beyond measure, but that doesn't have to stop us from exploring every available facet and knowing as much of it as our brains can fathom.

"The Lord your God in your midst, The Mighty One, will save; He will rejoice over you with gladness, He will quiet you with His love, He will rejoice over you with singing."

Zephaniah 3:17 (NKJV)

GOD'S LOVE SONG

When you take a close look at this passage, it reveals a lot about God and His relationship to us. In Zephaniah chapter 3, God rebukes the sin of His people, encourages them to look for mercy and, ultimately, promises to restore them. Though this Old Testament verse is God's assurance of Israel's restoration, it is also meant for us. What a blessing to ponder each nugget of truth in these phrases.

The LORD is in your midst. (Zeph 3:17 NKJV) You can know that God is right there with you, ready to deliver you. If you ever feel alone, meditate on this verse. You're not forsaken or deserted. Your mighty God is present and will rescue you!

Beyond that, *He rejoices with gladness over you.* (Zeph 3:17 NKJV) He prizes you and is glad that you are His. There's something special about feeling special. When you recognize that God cherishes you, your faith will deepen.

He will quiet you with His love. (Zeph 3:17 NKJV) He treasures you SO much that His love gives you peace! There is no better example than that of a child quietly sleeping in his father's arms. Children feel safe and secure in the embrace of a loving father. When we accept our Father's unconditional love, peace will flood our soul.

I think the most amazing revelation mentioned is this – "*He will rejoice over you with singing!*" (Zeph 3:17 NKJV) God breaks into song – over YOU! That's how much He delights in you. Imagine the tender voice of your loving Father, emanating the sweet echoes of a love song, written just for you.

Take a breath and think about that.

Have you ever found yourself humming and not even realized you were doing it? We know in our personal experience, that jubilation generates the desire to sing.

We may picture angels singing in worship to God, and we sing our own songs of praise to Him, but here we are told that God, our heavenly Father, out of the joy in His heart over us, expresses a glorious melody.

No matter what your circumstances, take comfort in knowing - You are loved!

*"Stay in the city until you have been
clothed with power from on high."*

Luke 24:49 (NIV)

POWER TOOLS

Howard loved retirement. He enjoyed working on projects and loved spending time with his family. One Saturday morning, both of these pleasures occurred.

As Howard sanded a piece of wood, his son, Phillip, sat on a bench, bemoaning his latest struggle. "I've tried everything," he complained. "Nothing seems to work."

Howard continued building his latest project, and listened to his son's dilemma. Phillip was discouraged at the lack of enthusiasm in his youth group. As a youth leader, he wanted to "get through" to the teens, but after many attempts, he felt like a failure.

Giving ear to his son, Howard began assembling the sides of the birdhouse. Using a battery-operated screwdriver, he tightened the screws, easily joining the pieces. However, as Phillip described his numerous efforts in the ministry, Howard noticed a distinct whining sound in the screwdriver. He inserted the next screw and the battery died.

Phillip continued his lament, casually observing his dad work. Then he stopped talking. He watched Howard fumble with the electric screwdriver, trying to turn the screw *manually*. Howard rotated the power tool with a clumsy hand-over-hand motion, awkwardly twisting the screw. It was painful to watch, and Phillip gawked at the sight.

"Dad!" he finally exclaimed. "What are you doing?"

Howard looked up at his son. "What does it look like I'm doing?" he asked.

"Don't you have another battery?" he questioned, pointing to the charger on the workbench. Its LED light glowed green indicating a fully charged battery.

"Sure," Howard responded, "That would probably work better...but I'd like to keep trying this." Phillip grimaced. Then he noticed the hint of a smile on his dad's face.

"All your struggling in ministry looks like this, Phillip," Howard said calmly. "You complain that you're burnt out, but you've forgotten the most necessary thing."

Howard reminded Phillip about Jesus telling the apostles to wait for the Holy Spirit before starting their ministry. He shared from Paul's message to the Corinthians, *"My speech and my preaching were not with persuasive words of human wisdom, but in demonstration of the Spirit and of power."* (1 Corinthians 2:4 NKJV)

Without the power of the Holy Spirit, we can do nothing. Phillip smiled, lesson learned.

"Then the Lord said to Moses, "Make a
fiery serpent, and set it on a pole; and
it shall be that everyone who is bitten,
when he looks at it, shall live."

Numbers 21:8 (NKJV)

LOOK TO JESUS AND LIVE

Kathleen's health problem was unsettling. Being in full time music ministry with her husband and raising three small boys was enough to fill her plate. Now, with an undiagnosed ailment, the enemy seemed to be gripping her with apprehension. "If I only knew what's causing these symptoms, I could figure out how to treat it," she supposed.

Praying constantly for healing and relief, she waited on the Lord for an answer. One day, she swung open the door to her backyard and walked into a tree branch that hung in front of her. Suddenly she realized she was eye to eye with a snake. Way too close for comfort, she instinctively reeled back and shrieked. Her boys came running over to her, curious about what happened. She snapped a quick photo of it on her phone before it slithered away.

Her first thought afterwards was that God was trying to tell her something. However, being face to face with a snake was not what she expected. Without clarity, the incident sat tucked away in her mind.

A week later, Kathleen decided to ask for prayer publically, through her newsletter. It was the first time she openly shared about this trial she'd been suffering with for months.

The response of love and prayers was incredible. Yet, one reply in particular, took her breath away. "Kathleen, look at the bronze serpent and be healed, in Jesus name." What? Look at the serpent? Be healed?

Mesmerized by the words, it took a moment before she noticed there was a photo attached to the email. It was a picture of a snake lifted up on a stick, representing the "bronze serpent", but most amazing was that it looked identical to the photo she had taken in her backyard.

Immediately, she sensed the Lord nudging her spirit to keep her eyes on Him! Jesus said in John 3 that like the bronze serpent, He was lifted up so that all who believe in Him shall live.

Kathleen's answer had come in a powerful way. Keep your eyes on Jesus and live!

*"A man's heart plans his way, But
the Lord directs his steps."*

Proverbs 16:9 (NKJV)

A PERFECT PLAN

For 35 years, Paula worked as an administrative assistant for a large company. Without warning, the corporate office dissolved her department, abruptly leaving her and 90 other employees jobless.

Paula was devastated, having loved her job. She wondered what the future held. At 59, she was too young to retire and would need to find work. She decided to look for something very different from her office career.

She owned several cats and a horse, which prompted her to take a job at a grain store. There she met other animal lovers including a Christian woman who had recently been blessed with a horse. They became fast friends, taking opportunities to ride their horses together.

During their conversations, her friend asked Paula about her relationship with God. Having grown up in a traditional church, she questioned many of their religious teachings and rejected their meaningless rituals, leaving her spiritually empty. She left the church at 18, thinking she was a Christian because she believed in God and Jesus. She was missing the most important thing, a personal relationship with the Lord. However, she did believe that God had a plan for her.

Through the patient guidance of her friend, Paula began to understand what that personal relationship meant and was eager to learn more. She attended a church that taught the Scriptures and began reading the Bible. Soon, she accepted Christ into her life, making Jesus her Lord and Savior. Afterward, she was baptized to proclaim her newfound faith. Paula became a "new creation" and was so excited about her salvation she couldn't wait to share the good news with everyone.

After two years at the grain store, she was once again, unemployed. This time, she saw God working out a perfect plan. Her elderly mother required more assistance due to failing health. Without the responsibility of a job, Paula was able to care for her mom full time. In this last year of her mother's life, Paula ministered to her both physically and spiritually, assuring Paula of a heavenly reunion.

Recalling her corporate career cut short, she now sees the path that led her to Jesus. She knows without a doubt that God had been directing her steps!

*"For though we live in the world, we
do not wage war as the world does. The
weapons we fight with are not the weapons
of the world. On the contrary, they have
divine power to demolish strongholds."*

2 Corinthians 10:3-4 (NIV)

PRAYER SENTINELS

Corrie Ten Boom once told the story of a missionary who sat alone in his house one night; his life threatened by dangerous enemies. The next day, one of these enemies approached the missionary and admitted that he and three of his companions had planned to kill him. When the missionary asked why they didn't, the would-be assassin complained, "There were too many men around your house." In fact, he claimed that there were seventeen watchmen.

When the missionary wrote about the incident to friends in his home country, they were amazed. For on that very night, seventeen of them had gathered at a prayer meeting, upholding their brother in the faith. Their prayers mobilized a border of sentinels – angels, activated to protect the man of God.

Have you ever considered that your prayers are your greatest weapon? In Ephesians 6, Paul tells us that we are fighting against supernatural powers, not against flesh and blood. Therefore, we need to fight with spiritual weapons. After describing spiritual armor in verses 11-17, Paul declares, *"And pray in the Spirit on all occasions with all kinds of prayers and requests… always keep on praying for all the Lord's people. Pray also for me… so that I will fearlessly make known the mystery of the gospel… Pray that I may declare it fearlessly, as I should."* (Ephesians 6:18-20 NIV)

Paul knew that prayer was crucial ammunition against Satan. When Jesus' disciples failed to heal a demon-possessed boy, Jesus explained, *"This kind can come out only by prayer."* (Mark 9:29 NIV) Wow! Prayer is like a spiritual *nuclear* weapon.

Considering the scarcity of prayer meeting attendees, and the overall deficiency of Christians with a solid prayer life, I believe Satan has his strongest advances against the praying Christian. Prayer scares the enemy, so he will do whatever he can to keep you from praying.

Remember; *"The prayer of a righteous person is powerful and effective."* (James 5:16 NIV)

Every believer has access to this incredibly potent tool. Become a warrior on your knees, and watch the battle from the winning side!

"For the Lord does not see as man sees;
for man looks at the outward appearance,
but the Lord looks at the heart."

1 Samuel 16:7b (NKJV)

JUICY FRUIT

Ann and Mark had just moved into their newly purchased home. Having spent their lives in New England, they noted that North Carolina certainly had a different environment. The warmer climate enabled many fruit bearing plants and trees to flourish.

They decided to explore their large backyard, excited that the former owner cultivated numerous fruit trees and several nut-producing trees. However, as Ann walked along the side of the garage, she noted two ugly bushes. With oversized leaves and disproportionate branches, the unsightly shrubs would surely have to go.

While she and her husband contemplated their demise, a woman from next door approached, wanting to welcome them to the neighborhood. She happily informed them of all the wonderful fruits they had on the property. "Y'all got persimmons and pears in the front yard," she pointed out with her sweet southern drawl. "And oh, you can't overlook these beauties," she said as she reached into the ugly bush.

Pulling out from between the leaves a dark purple bulb, she declared, "Figs!" Then carefully tearing the fruit in two, she gave Ann one half and ate the other. Sweet! Ann was amazed.

Have you ever been misjudged? It's disheartening to have someone think something wrong about you because of what they don't know. Yet, how often do we do the same thing.

Grace had xeroderma pigmentosum. Her skin was extremely sensitive to the sun. Any direct exposure would result in blisters. Grocery shopping meant wearing a long sleeve shirt, gloves, sunglasses and a large brimmed hat to shade her face. Parking in the handicap spots allowed her to get inside quickly. However, because she appeared healthy and hurried inside, many people scowled at her, thinking she swindled the handicap permit.

It's amazing how quickly we can come to a wrong conclusion by looking at something superficially. What we assume may not at all be accurate.

If the love of Jesus is to shine through us, we need God's perspective on those around us.

Ask the Holy Spirit to fill you with compassion that looks beyond the exterior and recognizes that God changes hearts. Then, like Ann, you may discover some juicy fruit!

"Charm is deceitful and beauty is passing, But a woman who fears the Lord, she shall be praised."

Proverbs 31:30 (NKJV)

REAL BEAUTY

Hailey surged with a mix of emotions. She spent time and money helping a friend who barely had enough to buy food. Then her friend told her that she had just gotten her hair colored for sixty dollars.

Hailey's outrage quickly turned to criticism. "How could she blow that much money in a salon?" She was unsympathetic, but then she felt God appealing to her heart. How much time and money did she spend on her own looks? His voice was not condemning, but gentle, unveiling the ugliness in her judgmental attitude.

The incident gave Hailey a reason to examine her own motives. The critical attitude toward her friend was based on her own limited knowledge of the situation. It wasn't Hailey's call to judge whether her friend's choice was wrong. That was between her and God.

Sadly, we live in a world where outward beauty equates to worth and a person is valued by how they look. That is not how

God sees things, and neither should we. 1 Peter 3:3-4 says, *"Your beauty should not come from outward adornment … Rather, it should be that of your inner self, the unfading beauty of a gentle and quiet spirit, which is of great worth in God's sight."* (NIV)

Statistics show that enormous amounts of money and time are spent on beautifying products and procedures, including make-up, hair products, nail and facial spa treatments and even drastic cosmetic surgeries.

When we obsess over our appearance, we make it an idol and it becomes sin in our life. Yet, it is perfectly acceptable to want to look our best! Wearing make-up or coloring your hair is not wrong, but as Paul told the believers in Romans 12:2 *"Do not be conformed to this world, but be transformed by the renewing of your mind."* (NKJV)

The world may push "glamour" and "style" at us, but God's Word clearly tells us to reject that influence. Real beauty is what God makes of us.

Paul's advice is to, *"Set your minds on things above, not on earthly things"* (Colossians 3:2 NIV). If we make Christ our focus, our appearance will take a back seat. After all, whom are we trying to impress?

"We also thank God without ceasing, because when you received the word of God which you heard from us, you welcomed it not as the word of men, but as it is in truth, the word of God, which also effectively works in you who believe."

1 Thessalonians 2:13 (NKJV)

SPECIAL EFFECTS

That title probably has you thinking of a Sci-Fi movie with plenty of visual illusions. However, there's a special effect that takes place in Christianity and it is a direct result of God's Word.

1 Thessalonians 2:13 says that God's Word *"effectively works"* in those who believe. That phrase literally translates - *energeō* where we get our word energy. It means to *"be active"*, "effectual" and "be mighty in".

In other words, the Bible is powerful to change lives. Hebrews 4:12 says, *"For the word of God is **living and powerful**, and sharper than any two-edged sword, piercing even to the division of soul and spirit, and of joints and marrow, and is a discerner of the thoughts and intents of the heart."* (NKJV emphasis added)

When you read God's Word, believing it is the Truth, it

becomes a powerful tool to change you. Unlike books written by men, the Bible does more than enlighten, educate or entertain. As the Word of God, it has the ability to transform our lives with Christ-like characteristics.

Psalm 19:7-9 says that it revives our souls, makes us wise, gives joy to our hearts and gives light to our eyes.

For those that disagree, Spurgeon put it this way, "That you have not perceived spiritual things is true; but it is no proof that there are none to perceive. The whole case is like that of the Irishman who tried to upset evidence by non-evidence. Four witnesses saw him commit a murder. He pleaded that he was not guilty, and wished to establish his innocence by producing forty persons who did not see him do it. Of what use would that have been? So, if forty people declare that there is no power of the Holy Ghost going with the word, this only proves that the forty people do not know what others do know." (Three Sights Worth Seeing, March 24th, 1887, by C. H. Spurgeon)

God's Word can do a work in you, but it means you need to be reading it. Read on and see what special effects He produces in you!

"The will of the Lord be done."

Acts 21:14b (NKJV)

THE POWER OF A COMMA

During one of Paul's missionary journeys, he encountered a time when the believers tried to discourage him from going to Jerusalem. Although it was his heart's desire, he knew going to Jerusalem would mean imprisonment.

In Acts 21:11, a prophet named Agabus, *"took Paul's belt, bound his own hands and feet, and said, "Thus says the Holy Spirit, 'So shall the Jews at Jerusalem bind the man who owns this belt, and deliver him into the hands of the Gentiles.'"*(NKJV)

Hearing this, Paul's companions begged him not to go. Yet Paul responded, *"I am ready not only to be bound, but also to die at Jerusalem for the name of the Lord Jesus."* (Acts 21:13b NKJV)

Was Paul wrong to ignore the warnings of the Holy Spirit? Paul reveals who directed his journey in Acts 20:22-23, *"I go <u>bound in the spirit</u> to Jerusalem, not knowing the things that will happen to me there, except that the Holy Spirit testifies in every city, **saying that chains and tribulations await me.**"* (NKJV emphasis added)

How would you have reacted to his decision after pleading

with him not to go? Would you have walked away hurt because he did not heed your voice? His friends yielded; *"So when he would not be persuaded, we ceased, saying, 'The will of the Lord be done.'"* (Acts 21:14 NKJV)

They not only packed the bags, they went with him. They were not blindly following Paul; they were completely trusting God. Paul's friends ceased arguing and started traveling. They knew this was not a debate about sin, but the direction of the Holy Spirit in Paul's life. His friends considered that God had stopped Paul before on the road to Damascus. If necessary, God could do it again.

That should be our mindset. Like Paul's friends, we should remember that in spite of our opinions, warnings or recommendations, the will of the Lord be done.

When a spouse doesn't see things our way, or when an employer, teacher, coach or friend rejects our advice, perhaps our tendency is to remove the comma and change verse 14 from *"We ceased, saying, 'The will of the Lord be done.'"* (Acts 21:14 NKJV) to "We ceased saying, 'The will of the Lord be done.'" Oh, the power of that comma.

Contributing author: Nichole Smith

"And not only this, but we glory in afflictions also, knowing that afflictions work out patience,"

Romans 5:3 (MKJV)

WAIT TRAINING

In Romans 5:3, Paul makes an unusual claim. He says that we "glory" or boast in our affliction. I don't know about you, but when I'm afflicted, I don't typically brag about it! So what was Paul's point? The verse ends with the answer; *"afflictions **work out** patience"*. (Romans 5:3b MKJV)

The words "work out" got me thinking of a time when I was in high school. One of my teachers, a body builder who competed for the Mr. America title, asked me to do some artwork at his gym. I gladly agreed.

My assignment was to paint phrases on the walls. They were quotes designed to motivate and challenge the men as they worked out.

While working on the project, I witnessed a number of men daily pushing themselves to the brink. All of them, determined to reach a new weight goal, were constantly striving to lift a little more weight each time.

The job took only a few weeks to complete, but even in

that short time, I recognized changes in the guys I saw there regularly.

In James 1:2, we are exhorted to *"count it all joy when you fall into various trials."* (NKJV) Why? Because the testing will produce *patience.* The word patience is the Greek word *hupomone,* which at its root has the sense of enduring a heavy load.

Much like the body builders pushed themselves to lift their load to build muscle, God is doing the same in us with tribulation. Trials are a workout in "Wait Training". They build us up and strengthen us in spiritual maturity.

Grasping the idea that trials are a **good** thing isn't easy when we're in the middle of suffering. Often it's easier to complain and look for ways to get out of the trial. However, like those body builders, we need to remember the goal. The end result will make the workout worth it!

I also thought about the phrases I had painted on the gym walls. For the men who were ready to quit, one glance at a motivational slogan helped them refocus.

We, too, have our motivator, the Bible. It is God's wall of inspirational passages, designed to encourage and challenge us to press on.

*"We do not have a high priest who is
unable to empathize with our weaknesses,
but we have one who has been tempted
in every way, just as we are..."*

Hebrews 4:15 (NIV)

HE'S BEEN THERE

Ellie brushed a tear from her cheek, hoping little Mathew didn't see. He was whimpering as the nurse placed a Band-Aid over the needle site in his arm. The cold, sterile room was enough to induce anxiety in an adult, let alone a five-year-old. However, Ellie knew that her son was sick and drawing a blood sample was necessary to find out why.

Days later, Ellie and her husband were in the pediatrician's office. The diagnosis: Type I diabetes. At the doctor's announcement, a million questions swirled in Ellie's mind. How he got it, how to treat it, etc.

Overwhelmed, she barely heard the doctor explaining the treatment process. Despite his reassuring tone, the only words pervading her thoughts were *injections, strict diet* and *regular blood tests.* Her world was turning upside down. She envisioned needles - sharp, poking, stinging needles!

The drive home was quiet, each parent processing the blow. Ellie began to cry, but her sadness turned to anger. Questions now formed in her mind directed at God. *How could you let this happen? He's just a baby. Why, God?*

Doctors' appointments and lab work filled the next few weeks. Mathew drew braver with every visit, but Ellie still lacked peace. While sitting in a waiting room, Mathew playing quietly, Ellie's phone beeped.

"Praying for you, Sister. Jesus knows your pain. 2 Corinthians 1:5". She read her friend's text, wondering about the Scripture verse. In her Bible app, she input the reference. *"For just as we share abundantly in the sufferings of Christ, so also our comfort abounds through Christ."* (2 Corinthians 1:5 NIV)

Ellie ached for encouragement, but instead found herself disagreeing with the verse. *How can Jesus know my pain?* she thought. *He didn't have a sick child.*

Her eyes wandered to verse 3, *"Praise be to the God and Father of our Lord Jesus Christ, the Father of compassion and the God of all comfort."* (2 Corinthians 1:3 NIV) The word *Father* caught her eye and she was reminded that God the Father understood her pain as He watched His own Son suffer unto death.

She smiled with gratitude, as a supernatural comfort softened her heart.

"Though I walk in the midst of trouble,
you preserve my life. You stretch out
your hand against the anger of my foes;
with your right hand you save me."

Psalm 138:7 (NIV)

ANGEL IN WHITE

It's not hard to count our blessings as Christians, but how often do we think about the Lord's provision for us *before* we were His? God knows His own – even before we surrender to Him.

Joanne remembered a time, before Christ was in her life, as a young teenager. She and her friend were walking home late one night. The street along which they traveled was in a bad part of town so they strode briskly.

Suddenly, a car approached them, going in the same direction. As it slowed down, the girls heard a group of young men jeering. They continued walking, trying to ignore the boys' vulgar remarks. The car advanced at a crawl, keeping their pace as the obscenities continued.

"Don't look at them," Joanne stammered, as they quickened their steps, their hearts racing. After what seemed like forever, the car sped away. Joanne and her friend eased their momentum, nearly collapsing with relief.

Minutes later, they heard the sound of another car approaching from behind them. Their muscles tensed, but when they turned to the vehicle, Joanne's panic faded.

In a yellow Volkswagen, they beheld a woman dressed as a nurse behind the steering wheel. With her white cap and bleached white uniform, Joanne was sure she was glowing.

"You girls shouldn't be walking here," she called to them, and then offered, "Let me drive you home."

Flooded by an inexplicable peace, Joanne turned to her friend, "It's okay. Let's go with her." The woman drove them down the street, stopping at an intersection. "Look there," she said, directing them to look right.

There they saw the car that had passed them earlier. It was empty. With another glance, both girls were stunned to see the group of young men hiding behind a cluster of bushes. The two of them would have walked right past this point if not for the nurse's intervention.

Driving away, Joanne considered the sinister possibilities and a chill went through her.

As an adult, she recalls the incident with thankfulness for the Lord's divine protection and His kindhearted angel in white.

*"My brethren, count it all joy when you
fall into various trials, knowing that the
testing of your faith produces patience."*

James 1:2-3 (NKJV)

VICTIM OR VICTOR

It's hard to imagine a trial as something to celebrate. Yet, here, James is telling us to count it all joy. Does God expect us to be happy in our suffering? Is He telling us to enjoy our trials?

No!

This passage, like many throughout the New Testament, encourages us to rejoice when we go through trials, not because they are pleasurable but because they are profitable. The passage continues, telling us that the trials *produce patience*.

Our attitude will make all the difference in how we come through a trial. Some people will face a trial as a victim. As victims, they will often complain about their circumstances and blame others. They tend to run to people for sympathy and help and generally live in misery.

Sadly, victims focus on themselves instead of turning to God. They may pray to God to remove the suffering, but they don't see the trial as something beneficial.

Peter, who once tried to deter Jesus from going to the cross (Mark 8:32-33) said, *"Beloved, do not think it strange concerning the fiery trial which is to try you...but rejoice to the extent that you partake of Christ's sufferings, that when His glory is revealed, you may also be glad with exceeding joy"* (1 Peter 4:12-13 NKJV).

Each trial we face serves a specific purpose in our spiritual walk. In James' passage, the word "various" is from the Greek word *poikilos,* which translates; various colors, variegated, of various sorts. Like an artist, God will use different ordeals to create a beautiful masterpiece.

He may apply the dull gray undertones of disappointment or heavy red strokes of adversity. He might add the cold blue wash of loneliness or spackle our life with the drab brown hues of pain. Whatever comes, good or bad, He is painting a picture that in the hands of the Master will turn out beautiful.

However He chooses to paint our lives, we have a choice to yield our canvas to His brush strokes. When we embrace the suffering with patience, knowing that He is creating a treasure, we can emerge as victors and His signature will be visible to others.

*"I am the LORD; I will bring you out
from under the burdens of the Egyptians,
I will rescue you from their bondage, and
I will redeem you with an outstretched
arm and with great judgments."*

Exodus 6:6 (NKJV)

MY EXODUS

Determined to read through the Bible in one year, my husband found us a chronological reading plan. I was excited to get intentional and dig deeper, rereading passages I hadn't read in years. I've read the New Testament many times, but I couldn't say the same for the Old Testament – which is significantly longer. So, in January, we began. I read page after page, faithfully taking notes, trying to slow down, to ponder and absorb what I read.

Then I got stuck. I found myself skimming through pages of repetitiveness. The Old Testament chronicles Israel's past – and a pattern; they obey God, they move forward. They forget God, they worship idols. God allows them to experience the consequences of their actions, they cry out to Him for mercy, He saves them. Repeat.

Frequently, God tells the Israelites, *"I am the Lord your God, who brought you out of Egypt,"* (Exodus 20:2 NIV) No kidding, right? This was a huge part of their history for those that witnessed the miracles and for the children who heard the stories. Yet, it's repeated so many times.

I wondered how an entire nation could be so blind. For years, they literally followed a pillar of fire by night and cloud by day. I thought, God, where's my pillar of fire when I need guidance? I wouldn't fall astray if I saw the Red Sea part.

Then I heard a whisper in my heart. How many times had God come through for me and yet I still doubt Him? I sat still, meditating on that. How many times has God rescued me and I neglected to praise Him? How often have I journeyed in my *own* exodus and seen the miraculous changes and victories, yet my trust still wavers?

With holy conviction, I took these verses written in a different culture thousands of years ago and found significant personal meaning. Placing my name at the front and adding God's victory at the end, I found that I could have my own book of Exodus.

"[Name], I am the Lord your God, who pulled you out of [past issue/barrier/bondage]"

Contributing author: Christina Hicks

"I remembered my songs in the night. My heart meditated and my spirit asked: "Will the Lord reject forever? Will he never show his favor again? Has his unfailing love vanished forever? Has his promise failed for all time? Has God forgotten to be merciful? Has he in anger withheld his compassion?"

Then I thought, "To this I will appeal: the years when the Most High stretched out his right hand. I will remember the deeds of the Lord; yes, I will remember your miracles of long ago. I will consider all your works and meditate on all your mighty deeds." Your ways, God, are holy. What god is as great as our God? You are the God who performs miracles; you display your power among the peoples."

Psalm 77:6-14 (NIV)

A CURE FOR THE DOWNCAST

The psalmist starts out with a downcast spirit. He questions God. Much like we can do sometimes, asking "Why?" or "Where are you, God?"

But then he turns his thoughts to who God is. God is faithful, kind, good and loving. And as the psalmist meditates on the "wonderful works of God" he can say with confidence, "What god is as great as our God?"

Practically speaking, when we meditate on who God is, we too can find our downcast spirit turning bright. We can look back on what God has done for us and rejoice in those victories. And as we read His Word daily, we can see how wonderfully He worked in the lives of His people.

As we get to know Him, we find, like the psalmist, that God's ways truly are holy. As in all relationships, getting to know each other is crucial to a lasting love. When we get to know God and see His love for us, we will find ourselves falling in love with Him. That love will generate trust and lead to peace. That's why reading His Word is so important.

Recall what God has done. *"Praise the Lord, my soul, and forget not all his benefits."* (Psalm 103:2 NIV)

If you're feeling downcast, or the trials of life are causing you to question God, follow the path of the psalmist. Remember the deeds of the Lord and let His track record lift you up out of the mire.

*"I urge you, brothers... to offer your bodies as
a living sacrifice, holy and pleasing to God."*

Romans 12:1 (NIV)

AN EXCEPTIONAL ALTAR

An altar is not something we often consider. We usually picture
it in a church setting as a fixture, part of the décor. However,
altars are more than a piece of furniture. In the Bible, they
represented the seat of devotion.

By definition, an altar is an elevated table used as the focus
for a religious ritual, especially for making sacrifices or offerings
to a deity. Altars were a regular part of worship in the past. The
Old Testament speaks of sacrifices offered to idols and recounts
God's direction for the Israelites to offer sacrifices to Him. God
even gave specific instructions to the Israelites on how to build
the altar.

Today, we don't envision altars as a place of death. Yet,
that was their purpose. Sacrifice meant death. The worshipper
offered something – usually an animal, to the deity. The sacrifice
became a total loss to the devotee. Tragically, in some cultures
participants sacrificed their children. This was an abomination

to God and part of the reason He authorized the destruction of some nations.

God used the sacrifice of animals to show His people the seriousness of sin. Penitents would bring their offering, usually a lamb, to the altar, where the priest would slaughter it. This graphic picture would etch itself in the mind of the transgressor. "My sin caused this animal to die," they would ponder as the innocent lamb bled out.

Today, offerings to the gods of this world still take place, though the altars are not tangible objects. Individuals sacrifice their time and effort to acquire materials. The gods of money, power and sex still enslave their followers. Worshippers live for pleasure and reap the consequences of their sacrifices; addiction, STDs, unwanted pregnancy, loneliness, broken families. The loss is immense.

We all worship something. However, the liability differs when we worship the true and living God. We don't yield to our deficit, we yield to our gain. In fact, Christianity is the only theology whose Deity makes the sacrifice for the penitents. The cross is our altar – where Jesus sacrifice became the **final** offering for sin.

All He asks of us is to surrender our will to His. He does the rest!

"When evening had come, He sat down with the twelve. Now as they were eating, He said, 'Assuredly, I say to you, one of you will betray Me.' And they were exceedingly sorrowful, and each of them began to say to Him, 'Lord, is it I?'"

Matthew 26:20-22 (NKJV)

IS IT I ?

Have you ever felt unknown guilt?

I remember a movie where a young boy plays with matches in his father's warehouse and a cardboard box ignites. Frantically he snuffs it out with his jacket. He takes his matchbox and leaves the warehouse, sobered by what could have happened. In the middle of the night, his father receives a phone call. The warehouse is on fire. When the boy wakes up the next morning, he's told that the building burned to the ground.

With the box of matches and the singed jacket safely hidden away, he cringes from guilt. His father's business jeopardized by his foolish act. The shame was overwhelming, but fear silenced his confession. The story parallels the father's struggle to stay in business and the boy's tormenting guilt. Ultimately, he confesses to his father, showing maturity in his character.

In an emotional ending scene, the father forgives his son's misbehavior, but remarkably, he explains that the fire started by an electrical short circuit. The boy was not at fault for the fire, in spite of his reckless deed. Remorse tortured him throughout the movie, despite his innocence.

As sinners, we sometimes have unfounded guilt. When Jesus made the statement, *"One of you will betray me,"* (Matthew 26:20 NKJV) each disciple wondered if he were to blame, knowing his own weaknesses. I picture the scene this way: Jesus and the twelve, reclined at the table, enjoying the meal, talking quietly and Jesus suddenly declares his imminent betrayal. I'm sure the initial reaction was silence. Sadness flooding their thoughts, overwhelmed that someone would mistreat their hero. Then guilt seeps in, and then doubt. The questions begin, each man speaking just above a whisper, "Could it be me?"

Psalm 139:23-24 says, *"Search me, God, and know my heart; test me and know my anxious thoughts. See if there is any offensive way in me, <u>and lead me in the way everlasting</u>."* (NIV *Emphasis added*) Trust God to reveal your heart. Where there is sin, He is faithful to forgive, clearing your conscience.

"But He said, 'More than that, blessed are those who hear the word of God and keep it!'"

Luke 11:28 (NKJV)

NOT JUST ANOTHER SHOPPING TRIP

Melinda had one thing on her mind: a set of dishes. She finished browsing through the kitchen section of the department store, unhappy with the selections. As she started to leave, she sensed a strong prompting from the Lord to stay put!

Her first thought was "Why?" It didn't make sense. Then she thought, *maybe I've missed something, maybe the perfect dishes **are** here for me.*

She looked again down the display of tableware, still unsatisfied. Yet, the pressure to wait remained. Now she began to feel awkward, standing there pointlessly. The awkwardness increased when a young woman stepped into the aisle.

Melinda suddenly felt a sense of anguish on behalf of this stranger. She knew the Lord wanted her to talk to the woman. However, fear and doubt flooded her mind. She was the quiet type. Approaching a stranger was not easy for her.

She questioned whether the message really was from God, her mind wondering how this person would react.

In spite of her apprehension, her heart racing, Melinda approached the woman. "Excuse me," she began. "I know you don't know me, but I sensed the Lord telling me to ask you if you're okay."

The woman began to cry. Melinda asked her if she knew Jesus and her response was, "Yes, I'm a prodigal."

She shared that God was calling her back, but she felt ashamed. She thought going back to church would result in judgmental gazes and condemnation.

Melinda encouraged her from God's word. In the story of the prodigal, the father happily accepted back his son. "It's all about God's grace!" Melinda reassured this new acquaintance.

As soon as the word "grace" left her lips, the store's sound system began playing "Amazing Grace". Both women were now in awe! No doubt, God was at work in the heart of this prodigal. And for Melinda, being obedient to His prompting was crucial.

We may not always know the *whys* behind what God calls us to do, but when we're obedient, we can be sure the results will be awesome! For both Melinda and the prodigal, that was not just another shopping trip.

*"But I will sing of Your power; Yes, I
will sing aloud of Your mercy in the
morning; For You have been my defense
and refuge in the day of my trouble."*

Psalm 59:16 (NKJV)

HE IS MY SONG

Judy needed an operation. It was her first surgery and she sought the counsel of friends and family to enlighten her about the process, regarding pain and recovery. The search for answers turned into one horrible account after another. Each conversation revealed the horrors of individual experiences. Her peace began to fracture.

Maybe they were trying to prepare her for the worst, or they elaborated on the dreadful details hoping to magnify God's great deliverance. Regardless of their good intentions, Judy left each testimony feeling more anxious. The fear trickled in as she contemplated a painful recovery.

Two days before surgery, Judy received a call from the hospital. The pre-op nurse informed her that the recovery period included much pain and difficulty moving. Panic gushed in and Judy's peace had all but disintegrated.

The day before surgery, after having tossed and turned all night, she got alone with her Lord. Pouring out her fears and pleading for God's peace and strength.

God answered that prayer abundantly. She focused on His love and the fear evaporated. She experienced peace and had a song in her heart. Overjoyed by His presence, the next day she woke up singing His praises - right into the operating room.

Then came the post-op process. The singing had stopped. She complained and moaned that first rough and painful night. When morning came, the slightest movement exploded in agony. Getting out of bed was unbearable. Even her hopes in the pain medication dwindled.

Then Judy recalled the One who put a song in her heart just 24 hours earlier. She picked up her devotional and read the day's Scripture verse. *"God is in the midst of her, she will not be moved; God will help her when morning dawns."* (Psalm 46:5 NASB) Wow! Elated by God's direct reassurance, she had to hold back the laughter to prevent pain at her incision.

It was exactly what Judy needed to hear. Over the next few weeks, she drew strength and comfort from it, getting through the pain with God in her midst, and singing praises to His name.

"Here I am! I stand at the door and knock. If anyone hears my voice and opens the door, I will come in and eat with that person, and they with me."

Revelation 3:20 (NIV)

ONE ON ONE

Growing up with eight siblings made it challenging to find personal time with Mom or Dad. Interruptions came frequently and made it impossible for private conversation. At thirteen, I remember how special I felt when my parents took me out to dinner. It was the first time I had them all to myself.

They had to divide their time between their children. Thankfully, God doesn't. He can always meet with us.

When the children of Israel wandered in the desert, God provided manna for their food. He told them, *"Everyone is to gather as much as they need. Take an omer for each person you have in your tent."* (Exodus 16:16 NIV) An omer equaled one serving.

Later in the book of Leviticus, God gave instructions on the offerings in the Tabernacle. Chapter 24 verse 5 describes the showbread. *"Take the finest flour and bake twelve loaves of* *bread, <u>using two-tenths of an ephah for each loaf</u>."* (NIV Emphasis added) The loaves sat on the table of "showbread" (Exodus 25:30). The word literally means "bread of the face" suggesting its consumption in God's presence; eating with God.

There are some wonderful parallels in this passage.

First, these breads represented an ongoing meal offering, kept throughout the week. They remained on the table every day. God shows that He wants a daily communion with us. We need to seek Him **every** day, not just once or twice a week.

Secondly, they were replaced with fresh loaves each Sabbath. God wants us to refresh our communion with Him each week. He doesn't want our relationship to be stale, but desires a vitality in our fellowship with Him.

Thirdly, there were 12 loaves – one for each tribe – showing that there is plenty for everyone. Yet, it wasn't **one** big loaf, but individual loaves. God seeks us on an individual basis, which leads to my final point.

God commanded that each loaf have two omers of flour (*two-tenths of an ephah*). The breads were the perfect size for two. He wants to "break bread" with us. God wants us to have one-on-one time with Him.

*"But seek first the kingdom of God
and his righteousness, and all these
things shall be added to you."*

Matthew 6:33 (NKJV)

THE LORD WILL PROVIDE

When Rut and her husband adopted their first child, they explored the possibility for her to be a stay-at-home mom. Financially, it was inconceivable. Without Rut's income, they questioned how they would pay the bills. However, after prayerful consideration, Kemy made the decision; Rut would quit her job to be a full time mom. They would trust God for His grace and provision.

Two days later, doubt filled Rut's mind. So much was at stake. They still had all the usual bills, but now with a child there would be more expenses. Could this be what God wanted? She began to fret, worried about what would have to be sacrificed to make it all work.

Then she started rummaging through the pile of mail that had accumulated during their overseas adoption trip. Buried in the assortment of parcels, Rut found an envelope from their former credit card company. Curiously, she opened it and found a check for just under $2000 dollars. More than a decade ago, they overpaid interest on their account and this check was their reimbursement.

Instantly, Rut perceived God's message that He would take care of them!

In line with God's will, Kemy's decision made evident their Jehovah-Jirah, the God who provides. God knew their needs before they did, and He already had a plan to support them. That check was the first of many different means to take care of them. Through financial gifts, donated clothes and toys and Kemy's job, God continued to sustain them. Moreover, He provided for a second adoption.

Two years later, Rut looks back to see how they have never lacked anything. As they faithfully raise their sons, they look to their heavenly Father who generously cares for His children. Indeed, He is a good, good Father.

As His Word says, *"For your Father knows the things you have need of before you ask Him"* (Matthew 6:8 NKJV). He knows when our hearts line up with His, and He is well pleased when we seek to do His will.

If you struggle with trusting God for a decision, remember that where God guides, God provides. Rut and Kemy can heartily testify to that!

"Do not conform to the pattern of this
world, but be transformed by the renewing
of your mind. Then you will be able to
test and approve what God's will is—
his good, pleasing and perfect will."

Romans 12:2 (NIV)

SENSIBLE SEPARATION

The Biblical account of Joseph is an amazing testimony of faith. Genesis 37 tells the incredible story of the 17-year-old boy whose jealous brothers sell him into slavery. Chapters 39 through 48 relate his difficulties in Egypt and the fate of his family. There are many insights to gain by dissecting Joseph's life. We learn perseverance, patience, faithfulness, integrity, and humility, just to name a few. However, looking at the story with an expanded view reveals an even greater plan than the one on the surface, which was saving Israel from starvation.

God devised a plan for the Israelites to go to Egypt during the famine. He used the evil intentions of Joseph's brothers to set in motion His master plan. Not only did this plan allow the Hebrews to live during the famine, but also to prosper and grow as a nation.

"But," one might ask, "Why didn't God just produce food in Canaan? Why did He go through all this trouble to move Jacob and his family?"

If God had provided food in Canaan where Jacob was living, the Hebrews would likely have intermarried with the Canaanites. By exchanging in marriage with the relatively small group, the Canaanites would have absorbed the Israelites into obscurity. Essentially, Jacob's family would never have turned into the nation of Israel. This would have completely jeopardized the Messiah's line. No Hebrew nation - no Messiah - no salvation! That would have been a disaster!

Genesis 43:32 states that Egyptians would not eat with Hebrews. It was an abomination to them. Egyptians considered themselves racially superior. This intolerance barred them from intermarrying because it would pollute their bloodline. God knew this.

God placed Jacob's family in a country where they maintained separation. In effect, He sheltered them from mingling with the world. This preserved the Hebrew genealogy and line of the Messiah.

God wants us to be separate also. Romans 12:2 states, *"And do not be conformed to this world, but be transformed by the renewing of your mind,"* (NKJV) When we renew our minds with His Word, our transformed lives will affect this world for God's kingdom.

"Jesus answered, "I am the way and the truth and the life. No one comes to the Father except through me.""

John 14:6 (NIV)

SINCERELY HIS

We tend to think that sincere people always do what's best. In fact, most would say that sincerity is a prerequisite to integrity. Sincere people will express kindness, honesty and trustworthiness. However, even the most sincere person can be wrong. Sincerity is NOT an indication of truth.

This is evident in the story of our first President's death. George Washington had some of the most knowledgeable doctors of his day. These top-notch physicians admired him and in all sincerity did what they believed to be the best thing to help George get better. However, in his weak state, after having caught a terrible cold from being outside in the frigid rain, his doctors removed more than 80 ounces of his blood over a twelve-hour period. That is 40% of his total blood volume.

Though bloodletting was a common practice, it was detrimental, in spite of what the medical field professed. The Bible declares, *"Do not eat the blood, because the blood is the life"*

(Deuteronomy 12:23 NIV) and *"For the life of a creature is in the blood,"* (Leviticus 17:11 NIV). Had Washington's doctors read God's Word and believed what it said, maybe they wouldn't have bled him to death.

Sincerity does not get us into heaven. Many people adhere to erroneous doctrines, believing wholeheartedly that they are true. Like Washington's doctors, they may be sincere, but they are sincerely wrong.

So how do we know what to believe? Truth exists and it demands acceptance. 2 + 2 cannot equal 4 *and* 5. Like mathematics, theology has very definite truths.

With all the differing religious beliefs, one thing is certain: they can't all be correct. In fact, each system of belief is mutually exclusive. For instance, Islam denies Jesus as God incarnate while Christianity affirms it. Either Jesus is God or He isn't. Both can't be true.

The Bible is the only reliable source of truth. In it, Jesus claimed to be God and proved it through His resurrection. Only in Christ do we have eternal life. Even the most sincere person who doesn't follow Jesus is lost. No matter how genuinely they believe an untruth, it is still a lie.

*"For our light affliction, which is but for
a moment, is working for us a far more
exceeding and eternal weight of glory, while
we do not look at the things which are seen,
but at the things which are not seen. For the
things which are seen are temporary, but the
things which are not seen are eternal."*

2 Corinthians 4:17-18 (NKJV)

SUFFERING IN HIS SOVEREIGNTY

When I was diagnosed with Leukemia, I found a strength and peace from God that I couldn't explain. It caught my oncologist off guard, and left him wondering why I wasn't upset when diagnosed. It was the perfect opportunity to share the Gospel with him.

Suffering through chemotherapy was trying, but even at the worst, I found myself totally depending on God. When I was too weak to get out of bed, I knew I could at least read the Word. When severe joint pain had me awake throughout the night, I could pray.

Yet, the most powerful change in my life was seeing how

God used this devastating disease to help me be an effective witness to everyone around me.

As I share the gospel message, I find many people are receptive to my words – because they see that facing death does not cripple me. It exposes the reality of my faith and gives people a clear picture of my hope in Jesus.

Cancer is also a connection for me to others suffering; a woman dealing with a cancer diagnosis, a man whose wife died of breast cancer, an acquaintance who suffers from a chronic disease. All of these encounters were fruitful because I could share in their suffering. People are far more receptive to you when they know you understand their pain. Having cancer makes me approachable to those who want encouragement.

Of all the things we're promised in the Bible, suffering is the one thing we'd like to do without. *"For it has been granted to you on behalf of Christ not only to believe in him, but also to suffer for him."* (Philippians 1:29 NIV) When the Bible refers to this promised suffering it implies persecution more than illness. However, God can use our suffering, no matter what the cause, to refine us.

If you are suffering, remember God's sovereignty and ask Him for strength to serve Him in spite of it. He can do mighty things through a willing vessel.

"Peter said to Jesus, "Master, it is good for us to be here; and let us make three tabernacles: one for You, one for Moses, and one for Elijah"—not knowing what he said."

Luke 9:33 (NKJV)

TASTY FEET

I remember meeting a friend of mine for coffee. I was already sitting at a table, having gotten to the café earlier. She approached with a steaming mug in hand looking quite distressed. I asked what was wrong and she floundered for words. "While checking out, I commented to the cashier how she was glowing. Then asked her when she was due." "That was nice," I commented. "Yeah, right up until she said, 'I'm not pregnant'."

How embarrassing! I couldn't help giggling, but my friend was mortified.

I think it's safe to say that most of us have experienced "foot-in-mouth" syndrome at one time or another. For some people, it happens all too often, suggesting that maybe their feet taste good. Why else would they keep sticking them in their mouth?

Peter must have had a case of *tasty feet*. The Gospels recount a number of Peter's impulsive remarks: his hasty plea to walk on the water, then crying for the Lord to save him, his brash advice telling Jesus not to talk about suffering, and receiving rebuke in return, his boastful declaration that he would never deny Jesus, only to deny Him three times.

Peter was no doubt an impetuous and passionate man. It was evident at Jesus betrayal when he struck the servant of the high priest and cut off his ear. All of these indiscretions express Peter's desire to "be the man", but reveal his inability to do so.

In the story of the transfiguration, Peter suggests building three tents, one each for Jesus, Moses and Elijah. But the passage also states that Peter spoke - *"Not knowing what he said."* (Luke 9:33 NKJV) Fear and astonishment caught him off guard and he opened his mouth.

Peter was outspoken, yet God used that to His benefit. Once submitted to God, Peter went from indiscretion to inspiration.

We've all experienced times of thoughtlessness. Peter's example proves that we are all subject to impulsive behavior. But it also encourages us to persevere, knowing that Jesus wants to transform us. And He will continue to use us, just as He did Peter.

*"There will be terrible times in the last
days. People will be lovers of themselves,
lovers of money, boastful, proud, abusive,
disobedient to their parents, ungrateful,
unholy, without love, unforgiving, slanderous,
without self-control, brutal, not lovers of
the good, treacherous, rash, conceited, lovers
of pleasure rather than lovers of God"*

2 Timothy 3:1-4 (NIV)

WHAT IN THE WORLD
IS GOING ON?

One morning, Tracy became very discouraged after watching the news. It seemed like the world was literally falling apart. Images of catastrophic floods and earthquakes bringing devastation to life and land. People committing atrocities on their fellow man; murdering, cheating, abusing and using them. And all the while, shady politicians promising to make things better.

Her heart cried out to God, "Lord, what in the world is going on? I know you'll return someday, and I know you win in the end. But Father, I don't understand how you can let evil prevail."

Then she went to her Bible. It was a much needed time with God. There in bold letters, Tracy read the Psalm of the day - *"Be still, and know that I am God; I will be exalted among the nations, I will be exalted in the earth."* (Psalm 46:10 NKJV)

What a wonderful confirmation that God speaks through His Word!

Tracy felt an immediate peace that she could not explain. God, in His love, let her know that He is still in control. And He WILL be glorified by all, one day. As she read that Psalm she knew He was telling her personally to be still, the Hebrew word *"raphah"* which means to slacken, forsake, leave, let alone.

When we let the cares of this world fill our minds, they will consume us. We need to slacken our grip on these thoughts, to forsake our worry, and to leave behind the bad news.

How do we do that? As His children, we can **know** that God rules. No matter what is going on around us, our heavenly Father is still in control and we can have victory.

1 John 5:4 says; *"For everyone born of God overcomes the world. This is the victory that has overcome the world, even our faith."* (NIV)

The media may inundate us with bad news, but with Jesus we have the *Gospel* – the Good News!

"On the first day of the week, Mary Magdalene and the other Mary went to look at the tomb. There was a violent earthquake, for an angel of the Lord came down from heaven and, going to the tomb, rolled back the stone and sat on it …The angel said to the women, "Do not be afraid, for I know that you are looking for Jesus, who was crucified. He is not here; he has risen, just as he said. Come and see the place where he lay. Then go quickly and tell his disciples"… So the women hurried away from the tomb, afraid yet filled with joy, and ran to tell his disciples."

Matthew 28:1-8 (NIV)

COME AND SEE

The stone was rolled away not to let Jesus out, but to let these women in.

"He is not here; for He is risen, as He said." (Matthew 28:6 NIV) This phrase, "As He said," is a subtle reminder, a gentle rebuke. They should have known He wouldn't be there. He had told them He would rise.

Oh, how often I forget the promises of God! He vowed to

never leave me or forsake me. (Matthew 28:20) If I seek first the kingdom of God and His righteousness, all these things will be added. (Luke 12:31) Still, I come to Him weeping, doubtful and questioning. In spite of this, if I seek Him I know I will find Him. (Jeremiah 29:13)

The angel first said *"Come and see."* Secondly he said, *"Go and tell."* (Matt 28:6-7 NIV)

I must first get a clear vision of where the Lord lay. It's not until I see the work of the cross and His resurrection from the grave that I have a message to "go and tell."

Expecting to see nothing more than Jesus' lifeless body, in their time of discouragement, defeat, and confusion, these women rose up early. How much more, then, should I be willing to rise up early to seek the living Lord?

If you feel that you're in the dark, alone, discouraged, defeated or you just want to be used of the Lord, be like these women. Rise early and come. See where the Lord lay. For it was these who rose early that would be the first to understand and experience Resurrection Sunday.

Contributing author: Nichole Smith

"Trust in the LORD with all your heart
and lean not on your own understanding;
in all your ways submit to him, and
he will make your paths straight."

Proverbs 3:5-6 (NIV)

TRUST AND OBEY

Understanding God's providence is essential to trusting Him. We trust those we know have our best interest at heart, and are capable of doing what is necessary to keep us safe. I think back to the ultimate lesson in trust when my youngest son was two years old. He loved to climb and we often found him on tables, counters, and other high surfaces. Remarkably, he loved to jump from those heights into my arms, never fearing I would drop him. Of course, I had no problem catching his little body, but there was something profound about his faith in me.

One day, at the age of three, little Joshua scampered across the top of our camper. Somehow, he had reached the elevated ladder and climbed to the roof. He scurried gleefully along the edge of the vehicle, oblivious to the menacing 11-foot drop. My ten-year-old daughter signaled the crisis with a shriek, "Joshua's on the roof!"

My heart skipped a beat as I jumped into action. My fear was that seeing me approach would cause him to jump. While his siblings distracted him, I climbed the ladder and calmly called him over. He happily complied, allowing me to wrap my arm around him. I held him tightly as we descended to safety.

Like my toddler's precarious adventures, we too can put ourselves at risk. We make decisions outside of God's will that jeopardize us, and we find ourselves skirting danger.

I believe that God wants us to have the kind of faith in Him that says, "I know you'll catch me!" But, that same faith must be accompanied by obedience.

Faith is not a game we play with God; it's the essence in our relationship with Him that causes us to obey. Hebrews 11 tells us that faith led the great men of God to obey. Abel, Enoch, Noah and Abraham all followed God by faith, trusting in a heavenly Father's love and ability to sustain them.

How can you increase your faith? Knowing God through His Word. *"Faith comes by hearing, and hearing by the word of God."* (Romans 10:17 NKJV)

Then Jesus asked them, "When I sent you
without purse, bag or sandals, did you lack
anything?" "Nothing," they answered. He said
to them, "But now if you have a purse, take it,
and also a bag; and if you don't have a sword,
sell your cloak and buy one. It is written: 'And
he was numbered with the transgressors'; and
I tell you that this must be fulfilled in me.
Yes, what is written about me is reaching its
fulfillment." The disciples said, "See, Lord, here
are two swords." "That's enough!" he replied.

Luke 22:35-38 (NIV)

GOD SWORD/GOD'S WORD

This verse describes a scene at the last supper. Jesus, knowing He would soon be leaving His disciples, gives them a warning. Jesus wasn't calling them to war and weapons, at least not in the worldly sense. If that were true, He wouldn't have rebuked Peter for using the sword in the garden only a short time later.

He was warning them about their future, without His physical presence. He would no longer be walking with them as before, and Jesus wanted them to know about the hostile world they would face. The dangers ahead were real, and Jesus was making a clear point.

Readiness is always the mark of a good soldier, and Jesus wants His disciples to be ready and armed to battle the darkness of evil in this world.

As believers, we too are in a battle. 2 Corinthians 10:3-4 tell us, *"For though we live in the world, we do not wage war as the world does. The weapons we fight with are not the weapons of the world."* (NIV)

Because the battle is a spiritual one, it requires a weapon of a spiritual nature. Our sword is the Word of God. As any good soldier would do, we need to be training in the use of our number one weapon.

The sword is both a defensive and offensive weapon, and so too is our God's sword. It will protect us from the wiles of the devil and demolish strongholds. But it also has the power to change us. Hebrews 4:12 says that this sword *"is a discerner of the thoughts and intents of the heart."* (NKJV)

The war is real. Get ready. Take hold of the Sword be prepared to use it!

*"The Lord looks down from heaven on
all mankind to see if there are any who
understand, any who seek God."*

Psalm 14:2 (NIV)

"I'M REAL" - GOD

At the end of Hebrews 11:6 it says that God *"rewards those who
earnestly seek him."* (NIV) What a wonderful promise! Best of
all, God doesn't limit that assurance to adults. Seeking God
and being open to receive Him can come at a very young age.

As he said his bedtime prayers, four-and-a-half-year-old
Hank was sad. When his mom, Lindsey, asked him why, he
replied, "I can't see God. How do I know He's real?"

Lindsey asked him, "Can you see the wind?" "No," he
answered.

"But you know it's real because you can see what it does,
right?" Lindsey continued, "You know the wind is real when
you see the trees swaying and the leaves blowing. The same
goes for God."

As he contemplated his mom's explanation, Hank
brightened. Then Lindsey suggested that he pray and ask God

to reveal Himself. She knew God would be faithful to make His presence known to little Hank.

The next day, Hank witnessed the mighty hand of God in the nor'easter that ravaged his community. With gusts of 70 mph, the trees were reeling wildly and debris whipped through the yard. The storm was an instant reminder of his bedtime conversation.

By evening, the violent gales had disrupted electrical service, with fallen trees bringing down power lines. The outages were widespread and thousands of people were in the dark.

Hank sat quietly with his family, candlelight glowing throughout the house. "When will the lights come back on, Mommy?" he asked, feeling a little uneasy in the blackout. "Why don't you ask God to bring the power back?" she prompted.

In an honest prayer, Hank candidly asked God to turn on the lights. A moment later, the room was bright! Although the majority of their town was without power, a portion of Hank's neighborhood had electricity. Could it be that God was showing Hank that He is for real?

To a little boy who earnestly sought Him and whose heart was open to receive, God made Himself known in a powerful example of His love.

"Your love, Lord, reaches to the heavens, your faithfulness to the skies." (Psalm 36:5 NIV)

"It has been given to you to know the mysteries of the kingdom of heaven,"

Matthew 13:11 (NKJV)

HIDDEN MESSAGE

I remember as a child, playing "secret agents" and sending cryptic letters to my friends. We would make up our own codes and send messages that could not be deciphered without the key. As we played, there were always those on the outside, the ones who couldn't make sense of the written notes.

In the Bible, we read about Jesus' method of *encoding* spiritual truths. He spoke in parables: earthly illustrations that had a heavenly meaning. The symbolism in such familiar tales would be memorable and easy to recall.

Yet, these stories didn't always make difficult things easier to understand. Often, they became obscure revelations of God's profound truths.

After Jesus spoke a parable, we frequently see that the crowds failed to comprehend His point. Even His disciples missed the meaning, often asking Jesus for an explanation.

So why did Jesus speak in parables? In Matthew 13:10-11, after Jesus taught the parable of the sower, His disciples asked

Him, *"Why do You speak to them in parables?"* His answer was *"Because it has been given to you to know the mysteries ... but to them it has not been given."* (NKJV)

It was Jesus intention to *hide* the meaning from those who refused to listen to the Holy Spirit. Jesus knew that if He spoke plainly, those who rejected His words would in effect be hardening their hearts even more.

Spurgeon said, "The same sun which melts wax hardens clay. And the same Gospel which melts some persons to repentance hardens others in their sins."

Parables were God's instrument of mercy, to limit the unrepentant hearts from piling up more rejection. Yet they also proved to be an instrument of judgement as they made apparent those who denied God's truth. A good example is the parable of the tenants where the Pharisees knew Jesus was talking about them.

As believers, we are so blessed to be part of the "insiders" – knowing the mysteries of the kingdom. Jesus said, *"I will ask the Father, and he will give you another advocate to help you ... the Spirit of truth,"* who will *"guide you into all the truth."* (John 14:16-17, 16:13 NIV) The indwelling of the Holy Spirit is the "key".

"My God, My God, why have You forsaken Me?"

Psalm 22:1 (NKJV)

A CRY FROM THE CROSS

Shortly before Jesus died on the cross, a particularly agonizing scene is found in Matthew 27:46. *"And about the ninth hour Jesus cried out with a loud voice, saying, 'Eli, Eli, lama sabachthani?' that is, 'My God, My God, why have You forsaken Me?'"*(NKJV)

Jesus faced a separation He had never known before. God the Father turned His face away, as Jesus took on the sin of the world.

Was it not enough that He left the riches of heaven to be born into poverty? Was it not enough that He laid aside His royalty to live in obscurity? Was it not enough that He forsook His own glory to be mocked by those who should have worshiped Him? As He who knew no sin became sin for us, the wrath of the God's judgment left Jesus temporarily isolated from His Father's presence.

This painful scene may be the reason why Jesus asked the Father, *"if it is possible, let this cup pass from Me,"*(Matthew 26:39 NKJV) The scourging that ripped open His back, the thorns that punctured His skull and the nails that pinned Him to the cross were nothing compared to the anguish of losing fellowship with His Father.

Yet, His final cry was more than a show of personal agony. The words He cried were the first line of Psalm 22. In ancient times, before they were numbered, it was common to identify a Psalm by its first line. For those standing nearby who understood that, reading Psalm 22 would reveal numerous prophecies that were being fulfilled before their very eyes.

Psalm 22:7 *"All who see me mock me; they hurl insults;"* Matthew 27:39 *"Those who passed by hurled insults at him."*(NIV)

Psalm 22:8 *"He trusts in the LORD; let the LORD rescue him."* In Matthew 27:43 the chief priests say, *"He trusts in God. Let God rescue him,"*(NIV)

Psalm 22:16 and 18 *"They pierced my hands and my feet,";* *"They divide My garments among them, And for My clothing they cast lots."* Matthew 27:35, *"Then they crucified Him, and divided His garments, casting lots,"* (NKJV)

Could it be that Jesus final cry of agony was also a last chance to point out who He was to those willing to listen?

"Therefore I take pleasure in infirmities…
For when I am weak, then I am strong."

2 Corinthians 12:10 (NKJV)

WARNING: ILLNESS ALLOWED

Ian's diagnosis was cancer. However, the doctors were optimistic about a promising treatment. Anointed for healing at church, he was constantly lifted up in prayer. God was in control and Ian trusted Him completely. "The worst that could happen is I die," he professed, "And I'm ready when God calls me home." He meant every word.

Months later, he met a brother in Christ he hadn't seen for some time. This friend listened intently as Ian shared the news of his illness. Then he spoke up, "Don't let the devil fool you, Ian. You don't have to be sick."

His words sounded more insistent than encouraging. So Ian told him how he'd been anointed for healing and that he believed wholeheartedly that God *could* heal him, declaring, "I will accept whatever God has for me."

At this point, his friend admonished him. "God does not want us to be sick. If we are sick, it is **our** choice to rebuke

Satan's attack and claim healing." Ian was speechless. He continued listening while his friend went on to explain that sickness was a ploy of the devil and no Christian should ever be sick. He urged Ian to stop allowing Satan to have his way, quoting, "By His stripes you are healed."

When Ian asked, "Can I expect to live forever?" His friend answered, "No, but disease should never take Christians."

The following day, Ian studied the Bible regarding sickness. His friend had been following the teaching of a Word of Faith preacher. This ideology claims that our faith is the instrument that keeps us healthy and illness fundamentally signifies a lack of faith.

Are we to expect that Paul's faith wasn't enough to cure his "thorn in the flesh"? in fact, the lives of Job, Paul and Timothy contradict this teaching.

In John 9:1-3, Jesus explained that a man was blind from birth so that, *the works of God might be displayed in him."*(NIV) God can use sickness for His greater purpose.

Sickness is part of living in a sinful world. We may face suffering here on earth, but we can choose to trust God in the midst of our infirmities, and like Ian, bring Him glory!

"I am the light of the world. He who
follows Me shall not walk in darkness,
but have the light of life."

John 8:12 (NKJV)

LIGHT AND LIFE

Years ago, there was an explosion at a mine. The cave-in left a dozen men waiting in darkness for the rescue team. They couldn't see in the pitch black, but the foreman called out the name of each worker asking if they were okay. One by one, they reported minor injuries. Amazingly, they all survived and each man seemed fine. As they huddled together, encouraging each other, the rescue team dug at the wall of gravel.

After hours of waiting, the miners cheered when a beam of light signaled their freedom. However, one man remained quiet and confused. "Are they through?" he asked. His coworkers looked at him, light now flooding the cave. Their friend was still fumbling in darkness, having been blinded by the explosion.

When they were all in the dark, no one knew he was blind; the fact is, the light revealed his blindness. Ephesians 5:13 says, *"But everything exposed by the light becomes visible—and everything that is illuminated becomes a light."* (NIV)

God's light in believers helps win the lost for Christ. *"I will also make you a light for the Gentiles, that my salvation may reach to the ends of the earth."* (Isaiah 49:6b NIV)

It also sanctifies the believer. As 1 Corinthians 4:5 says, the Lord will *"bring to light what is hidden in darkness and will expose the motives of the heart."* (NIV)

Light can be painful. As a photographer, I often spent hours in my darkroom. Many times, I would emerge into a brightly lit room, eyes squinting, adjusting to the light's intensity. It was harsh until my vision became acclimated.

So, too, is the light of the Spirit when it comes to sin. Whether to an unbeliever or to a child of God, light reveals our wickedness and can be uncomfortable. However, it is also necessary to bring salvation and sanctification.

Paul testified of his own experience on the Damascus road. The light of Christ made him physically blind, yet that same light gave him true spiritual sight. The light that converted Paul radically transformed him into the greatest missionary of all time. Let's take his advice and *"shine as lights in the world"* (Philippians 2:15 NKJV)

"I sought the Lord, and He heard me,
And delivered me from all my fears."

Psalm 34:4 (NKJV)

TAKE COURAGE

Mary's dad was ill, the prognosis grim. Despite her nursing background, she was unsure of his condition due to him being in Ireland. She and her husband, Frank, had shared Christ with her dad, but he had yet to accept Jesus. Now, as his physical life hung in the balance, his spiritual life became more concerning.

As Mary sought the Lord for wisdom, it became evident through His Word and her husband's encouragement that she needed to go see her father. God was calling her to share again the way of salvation with her dad.

However, that meant an overseas trip. Alone.

Fear emerged. She wasn't worried about sharing Christ with him, but the thought of driving by herself was frightening. In Ireland, people drove on the opposite side of the road, making the ride a challenge for American drivers. On past visits, Frank had done all the driving. Furthermore, she was unsure of the way, and the route to her parent's house from the airport would take four hours.

She felt God was telling her to go and with a reluctant heart, Mary replied, "But, Lord…" Her anxiety escalated as the enemy taunted her with uncertainty. How could she overcome her fear of driving?

The Lord showed her that questioning His leading in her life indicated that she thought her ways were higher than His. She humbled herself before Him, going to His Word for comfort and He faithfully encouraged her with this: *"Be strong and of good courage; do not be afraid, nor be dismayed, for the Lord your God is with you wherever you go."* (Joshua 1:9 NKJV)

He was speaking directly to her, and she knew it. Excited, she wrote the verse on an index card and put it on the refrigerator. She memorized it and over the next few weeks when the enemy tried to flood her with fear, she went back to God's promise and held firm. He would be with her!

Mary made the trip to Ireland and God accompanied her throughout the journey. She planted a seed with her dad that took root. To God's glory, her dad accepted Christ and less than six weeks later was at home in heaven.

*"Abide in Me, and I in you. As the branch
cannot bear fruit of itself, unless it abides in the
vine, neither can you, unless you abide in Me."*

John 15:4 (NKJV)

HANG IN THERE

Quite often, I've heard the term "bearing fruit", but what exactly does that mean? Obviously, we're not trees with fruit hanging off our appendages. That would be silly. Yet, in John 15:16, Jesus says, *"I chose you and appointed you that you should go and bear fruit, and that your fruit should remain…"* (NKJV)

So what exactly is it to bear fruit? What is fruit? Galatians 5:22-23 says *"But the fruit of the Spirit is love, joy, peace, longsuffering, kindness, goodness, faithfulness, gentleness, self-control."* (NKJV)

The interesting thing about fruit is that it does not exist for itself. All too often I want the fruit of the Spirit in my life so that *I* can be satisfied. However, the truth is, the fruit is not there for me to enjoy, any more than an apple tree enjoys its own apples. No, the purpose of producing fruit is that it may nourish others. Fruit is produced by the Spirit in us, through us and often *in spite* of us! Focusing on yourself brings misery. Be a lover of God and others and you will find complete satisfaction.

Now that we have defined fruit, what is the secret of fruit-bearing? In the above passage, Jesus said, *"Abide in Me."* (John 15:4 NKJV) Abiding is the secret and simply means to hang in there. Suppose I wanted to enjoy fresh apples all year long, so I went out and cut off the branch of my favorite apple tree to hang in my house. That would be ridiculous. Everyone knows that the branch cannot bear fruit unless it is attached to the tree. Christ is asking us to stay close to Him. If we cut ourselves off from Him in any way, we won't bring forth fruit.

Look at an apple tree, you'll notice the branches securely attached. You won't hear them grunting, or see them sweating, yet, as Christians we often strain and strive to bear fruit? We fail to understand that it is spending time with Jesus that allows Him to work through us.

The Spirit produces fruit in us as we remain with Jesus. The key: hang in there with Jesus and see what blossoms.

Contributing author: Nichole Smith

"He said to them, 'How foolish you are, and how slow to believe all that the prophets have spoken! Did not the Messiah have to suffer these things and then enter his glory?' And beginning with Moses and all the Prophets, he explained to them what was said in all the Scriptures concerning himself."

Luke 24:25-27 (NIV)

MESSIAH 101

There's no Bible study I would have desired to attend as much as the one Jesus taught on the road to Emmaus. (Luke 24:13-35) After a rollercoaster of events, two disciples walked in confusion after having seen Jesus crucified to having heard of His resurrection.

I love how Jesus **meets** them. *"As they talked and discussed these things with each other, Jesus himself came up and walked along with them;"* (Luke 24:15 NIV) He doesn't jump in front of them and reveal Himself, showing that He was alive. Instead, Jesus meets them with an unassuming presence, His identity hidden.

Then, He **connects** with them by simply asking, *"What*

are you discussing together?" (Luke 24:17 NIV) Bewildered that this stranger is unaware of the recent events, the two travelers open up to Him about their confusion and doubt, *"We had hoped that he was the one who was going to redeem Israel."* (Luke 24:21 NIV)

Now that communication is established, Jesus **teaches** them. He begins, *"How foolish you are,.."* (Luke 24:25 NIV) Here I picture a gentle reprimand, and then Jesus expounding on the Scriptures that point to a suffering Messiah. This was far from the regal prince they expected. Yet their hearts burned within as this stranger made sense of what had appeared to be senseless.

Like these two disciples, we can often walk in doubt and confusion, especially in the midst of tribulation. On these journeys, Jesus is sure to **meet** us, unpretentiously walking alongside us, waiting for us to recognize His presence.

Once we acknowledge Him, He may ask us what is wrong. Here's where He **connects** with us, as we pour out our hearts in an honest prayer.

That's when Jesus begins to **teach** us. Just like the lesson on the road to Emmaus, Jesus points to the Word. Jesus chose to bolster the faith of these two disciples with the Scriptures, *before* He revealed Himself. How critical for us, then, to do the same. For the testimony of Scripture is the basis of true faith.

"For the Lord God is a sun and shield; The Lord will give grace and glory; No good thing will He withhold from those who walk uprightly."

Psalm 84:11 (NKJV)

PERFECT PROVISION

Close to ten years in full time ministry was both challenging and rewarding, but now Nichole was back home. Through this season of experience, she acquired wisdom and knowledge, along with a cat and a dog. Coming home would carry its own challenges, one of which would be getting a job.

Being in ministry taught Nichole a lot about depending on God, and this pursuit would be no different. With complete trust, she settled in, knowing her heavenly Father would work things out.

A few weeks after reuniting with Nichole, a close friend informed her that an acquaintance was looking to hire someone to train dogs. This friend knew Nichole's skill with animals, and she mentioned it to her associate.

Nichole was excited about the idea of dog training. Her years as a horse trainer prepared her for such a career, and she had already worked wonders with Pearl, her beautiful border collie.

"My God shall supply all your need according to His riches in glory by Christ Jesus." (Philippians 4:19 NKJV)

When she met with the business owner, he was ready to hire her, knowing she was proficient at training horses. "When can you start?" he replied after becoming acquainted at their first meeting.

As she drove home, Nichole thought, "Wow, Lord! I didn't ask for it, but this job is perfect." Not only did God provide her with a job she could truly enjoy, but also the hours were perfect. Even more amazing was that she would be working in her hometown.

God always keeps His promises. As Paul told the Ephesians, we too can know; *"Now to him who is able to do immeasurably more than all we ask or imagine, according to his power that is at work within us, to him be glory in the church and in Christ Jesus throughout all generations, for ever and ever! Amen."* (Ephesians 3:20-21 NIV)

If you are waiting on God for something, remember that He is capable to provide perfectly for you. So, *"Seek first the kingdom of God and His righteousness, and all these things shall be added to you."* (Matthew 6:33 NKJV)

"For it is God who works in you to will and to act in order to fulfill his good purpose."

Philippians 2:13 (NIV)

DESPITE OURSELVES

It was a warm July morning when Rich began repairs at the convenience store. As an upkeep manager for the franchise, he kept busy with maintenance. At one location, he was finishing a project when he found new work to do.

As he went out to the parking lot to retrieve tools from his truck, he noticed two men in a vehicle next to his. He thought they looked distressed, but he headed back into the air-conditioned store to continue with his next task.

An hour later, he headed back outside for more tools. He opened the door to the sweltering heat and went to his truck. Once again, he saw the two men. This time, they were working under their car.

Rich felt a tug on his heart. The thick muggy air and scorching sun were oppressive. *These guys must be miserable,* he thought. Then he heard a still small voice tell him to get them something cold to drink. Back in the store, he got two refrigerated beverages. When he returned, however, doubt and fear cautioned him, *this is a bad neighborhood.* The warning deterred him from approaching the men, so he went back to work.

Rich was torn as he muddled over his decision. Once again, compassion moved his heart. He returned to the men with work-gloves and a mat to lie down on while they serviced their car. Their gratefulness made him happy that he helped, but he was disappointed that he withheld the drinks earlier.

Ready to head to his next location, Rich sat in his truck when one of the men came to the window. "Thanks again for helping us out, I want to give you something that may help you out," he said, handing Rich a Gospel tract and inviting him to church.

Grinning, Rich told the man he was already a Christian and the man turned to his friend, "Hey Pastor, he's already saved!"

Rich then handed them the cold drinks and told them how he had neglected to respond previously. They just smiled and answered, "God always provides!"

Rich discovered that God could use him, in spite of himself and he was glad God did!

"He came to Nazareth … And.. went into the synagogue on the Sabbath day, and stood up to read. And He was handed the book of the prophet Isaiah. And when He had opened the book, He found the place where it was written: "The Spirit of the Lord is upon Me, because He has anointed Me to preach the gospel to the poor; He has sent Me to heal the brokenhearted, to proclaim liberty to the captives and recovery of sight to the blind, to set at liberty those who are oppressed; to proclaim the acceptable year of the Lord." Then He closed the book, and gave it back to the attendant and sat down.… And He began to say to them, 'Today this Scripture is fulfilled in your hearing.'"

Luke 4:16-21 (NKJV)

THE PROLONGED PAUSE

In this passage, we find Jesus preaching in His hometown synagogue. He reads a portion from Isaiah, which talks about the Anointed One. It was a Messianic prophecy that pointed to the redemptive work of Christ.

Jesus only read the first two verses of the chapter. In fact, He stopped in the middle of verse 2. The final words of His reading – *"to proclaim the acceptable year of the Lord,"* (Isaiah 61:2a) allude to the year of Jubilee, when all debtors and slaves are set free. Then Jesus closed the book and proclaimed that He was the fulfillment of that passage. This declaration revealed both the person and the timing of Isaiah's prophecy.

Jesus wasn't coming to bring judgement, as the second part of verse 2 states; *"And the day of vengeance of our God."* (Isaiah 61:2b) The portion of Isaiah that follows goes on to talk about what the Messiah will do at His <u>Second Coming</u>. That's why Jesus didn't elaborate on it. He spoke of what was relevant to where He was at that moment, in His first coming.

Jesus refers to the anointing of the Messiah to heal the five plights of sin.

Sin brings poverty, but He brings the good news.

Sin breaks hearts, but He restores them.

Sin enslaves, but He liberates.

Sin blinds, but He gives sight.

Sin oppresses, but He rescues.

For over two thousand years, he has continued to minister in this way. Between the "a" and "b" of Isaiah 61:2 is one **long** pause!

*"Then the veil of the temple was torn
in two from top to bottom."*

Mark 15:38 (NKJV)

TORN APART

When we think of tearing apart something, it leads to thoughts of violence. I imagine a National Geographic episode where the predator gets the prey. Not a pretty sight!

The veil of the temple was a massive curtain that separated the Holy Place from the Holy of Holies, where the mercy seat of God dwelt. At sixty feet high, thirty feet wide, and as much as four inches thick, this was one heavy-duty curtain. Some commentators claim it took 300 priests to handle it, and that a yoke of oxen couldn't pull it apart.

The purpose of the veil was to keep sinful people from entering into God's presence. Isaiah 59:2 says, *"Your iniquities have separated you from your God."* (NIV) The perfect holiness of God cannot exist with sinful man, without unleashing wrath. Therefore, the veil was a boundary that protected the people and reminded them of their wickedness.

The high priest was the only one allowed to enter the Holy

of Holies, and that was to offer the yearly sacrifice to atone for the sins of the people.

When Jesus died, the veil was "torn"; taken from the Greek the word "schizō", which means to "rip, rend, or violently tear asunder". Torn from top to bottom, this rending started from above, with God forcefully severing the curtain in two.

This wasn't just a powerful assault on an inanimate piece of drapery, but rather the destruction of an object that shielded us from our Creator. A representation of our sin, the veil prevented access to Him.

Like the rending of the veil, Jesus was torn apart – beaten, scourged, nailed to a cross and forsaken by His Father – for the same reason: to grant access to God.

Jesus willingly sacrificed Himself on the cross, a new symbol of God's mercy, which replaced the Temple's mercy seat. The cross would be the final place where the holy blood of God's sacrificial Lamb was spilled, settling once and for all the debt of sin.

God no longer dwells behind a curtain, but is open to all who choose Him through Jesus. If you feel disconnected from the Lord, make sure you're not mending the curtain with self-condemnation or stubborn unbelief. His door is always open!

"And my God shall supply all your need
according to His riches in glory by Christ Jesus"

Philippians 4:19 (NKJV)

DIVINE ENCOUNTERS

Nancy was stunned. News of her mother's passing left her feeling numb, and with all the funeral arrangements, there was no time to mourn.

She and her siblings started at the funeral home and then went their separate ways to finalize the preparations. Her brothers went in one direction and she and her sister went back to her house. They were ready to head out on another errand when Nancy's husband answered a knock at the door.

There in the hallway, stood a precious sister-in-Christ. She came to offer comfort and prayer to their family. Encouraged by the kindness, Nancy told her sister how grateful she was at the thoughtfulness of her friend.

Back on the road, Nancy and her sister tackled more of their "to-do" list and by late afternoon, realized they hadn't eaten all day. Deciding on a nearby Chinese restaurant, they parked the car and made their way across the lot. As they approached the entrance, Laura, another friend from church, exited the building. Without hesitation, Laura offered her condolences and a sweet prayer of comfort to Nancy and her family. Nancy felt God's soothing touch.

After a quick bite to eat, Nancy and her sister went to get one last item. When they entered the department store, there was Julie, Nancy's Bible-study leader, standing right in front of them. Julie greeted them and after being introduced to her sister, they had a warmhearted conversation about their moms and how the Lord works.

There, in the middle of the store, Nancy and her sister once again heard a gracious prayer offered on their behalf. Julie's tender petition brought them solace.

After Julie left, Nancy froze, stunned by this divine incident. As she gazed in wonder, her sister asked if she was okay.

"Do you see what is happening?" Nancy answered, "Three times today, God brought my sisters-in-Christ to us, offering condolences, words of comfort and prayer." She added, "In the past year, I've never bumped into anyone from church, yet today, three dear friends have crossed our path!" It was no coincidence!

In blessing Nancy this way, God was also revealing Himself to her sister, who stood speechless. What she had witnessed that day was truly divine.

"For since the creation of the world His invisible attributes are clearly seen, being understood by the things that are made, even His eternal power and Godhead, so that they are without excuse."

Romans 1:20 (NKJV)

UNMISTAKABLE

By God's grace, science is beginning to see just how incredible the creation is, and how unquestionably it came from a Creator. It's far more difficult now to argue against intelligent design, than years ago. With the discovery of DNA, it takes a lot more faith to believe that it all "just happened" over time, by random chance.

One discovery in particular seemed to permeate Christian circles not too long ago. Laminin, discovered in 1979, refers to a family of proteins. One of their primary functions is to bind tissues and organs.

Interestingly, one article described it as a "cruciform shape", with two short arms extending from a longer rod, basically shaped like a cross. This is what spring boarded Christians to use laminin as an example of Colossians 1:17, *"He is before all things, and in him all things hold together."* (NIV)

It didn't take much to find illustrations of the laminin protein and note it's "t" shape. Yes, it looks like a cross and as a believer that put a smile on my face. But, equating this cross shaped discovery as a "sign" from God is a bit of a stretch. In fact, the protein is not a two dimensional object, and does not always present itself cross-shaped as the science books display.

Aside from that, though, is the simple fact that laminin is yet another incredible discovery from biology that shows God's incredible design. Regardless of its shape, Laminin is one more piece of evidence in a sea of countless proofs for creation.

We don't need to look beyond the incredible designs in nature to know that God exists, and we don't need to use the shape of the cross to prove that point.

Just as the intricate details in a finely woven tapestry or the impressive handiwork of a lofty cathedral point to the craftsman, all of nature points to the Creator. Though His likeness and power are "invisible", His existence is "clearly seen" in His creation.

"Clearly seen" comes from the Greek word *kathoraō* which means, "to behold fully". When we observe the world around us, there's no mistake about it!

"Do not remember the former things, nor consider the things of old. Behold, I will do a new thing, now it shall spring forth; Shall you not know it? I will even make a road in the wilderness and rivers in the desert."

Isaiah 43:18-19 (NKJV)

A NEW THING

We all appreciate the smell of a new car or the look of a new outfit. I remember, as a child, racing around in my new pair of sneakers. We can all appreciate a newly renovated room or house. New is fresh and pristine. In this world of entropy, where everything deteriorates over time, new is wonderful.

In the process of writing this book, I neglected to back up my computer, resulting in the loss of 6 months of work. Numerous devotions were suddenly gone.

My first reaction was disbelief. Then panic set in as I frantically searched for the missing folder. I gave the laptop to my son who fixes computers for a living. He thoroughly checked my hard drive, running a deep scan overnight. I was certain he would recover the files. Prayers went up as I continued to trust, believing that God was using this to test my faith.

Unfortunately, the next morning, my son informed me that he only recovered the file names. The documents were corrupted and inaccessible. To this day, I still don't know how they were "deleted" off my laptop.

After a good cry and many questions to my Father, I resigned to the fact that I would have to make the best of it. I stared blankly at the file names, which were the titles of each written devotion, thinking; *How could I ever rewrite all these pages?* My heart sank.

Still disheartened, weeks later, I happened upon Isaiah 43. Verses 18 and 19 gripped me. His words were like a whisper; "*I will do a new thing.*" (Isa 43:19) I wanted to protest, "The old pages were fine!" but His admonition was gentle. Accordingly, I laid down my will and accepted His. I am now sure God had a purpose in this.

The next day, as I looked through the titles once again, my mind flooded with remembrance. The Holy Spirit helped me rewrite almost all of the lost pages. Though I can't compare them, I know the new ones are even better!

*"Therefore let those who suffer according to
the will of God commit their souls to Him
in doing good, as to a faithful Creator"*

1 Peter 4:19 (NKJV)

ACCOMODATING
ADVERSITY

In his first book, Peter encourages us to persevere in suffering, then adds *"according to the will of God"*. (1 Peter 4:19 NKJV) This doesn't mean that God initiates the suffering, nor does He take pleasure in it. However, he does use it to accomplish His desire for our lives.

Romans 5:3-5 explains the usefulness of suffering; *"Not only so, but we also glory in our sufferings, because we know that suffering produces perseverance; perseverance, character; and character, hope. And hope does not put us to shame, because God's love has been poured out into our hearts through the Holy Spirit, who has been given to us."* (NIV)

As we are sanctified through suffering, we become more Christ-like. If Christ-likeness is the goal, than we need to learn to embrace suffering, rather than evade it. And *"Hope does not put us to shame,"* (Romans 5:5 NIV) because we have God's love in us through the power of the Holy Spirit.

It's more important to trust our soul to God. Psalm 23:1-3 states *"The Lord is my shepherd; I shall not want. He makes me to lie down in green pastures; He leads me beside the still waters.* **He restores my soul;"** (NKJV *Bold added for emphasis*)

Ultimately, the condition of our soul transcends external suffering. When we are completely trusting God, regardless of our circumstances, we live out a truer witness to who Christ is in our lives. We become a true reflection of God's transforming power.

There are two major benefits to suffering: transformation and manifestation.

We grow in strength and character as we endure hardship. Then our "attitude of gratitude" reveals a loving and faithful Father to those around us. This is only accomplished through the power of the Holy Spirit.

Matthew Henry reassures us; "By patience and fortitude in suffering, by dependence on the promises of God, and keeping to the word the Holy Spirit hath revealed, the Holy Spirit is glorified;- The only way to keep the soul well, is, to commit it to God by prayer, and patient perseverance in well-doing. He will overrule all to the final advantage of the believer." (An Exposition of All the Books of the Old and New Testaments, Volume 5, by Matthew Henry)

At the next sign of adversity, put out the welcome mat!

"Seeing then that we have a great High Priest
who has passed through the heavens, Jesus the
Son of God, let us hold fast our confession."

Hebrews 4:14 (NKJV)

TORN

Ann had been studying Jesus' role as High Priest and read about His trial before the Sanhedrin. Matthew's gospel tells us that Caiaphas, the high priest, asked Jesus directly, *"Tell us if You are the Christ, the Son of God!"* (Matt 26:63 NKJV) Jesus responded, *"It is as you said..."* (Matt 26:64 NKJV) Horrified by this reply, Caiaphas tore his clothes.

Interestingly, Leviticus 21:10 forbid the high priest from tearing his clothes. *"He who is the high priest among his brethren... who is consecrated to wear the garments, shall not uncover his head nor tear his clothes;"*(NKJV) The act of tearing one's clothes was a sign of mourning or extreme indignation.

The high priest was forbidden to rend his garments because he represented the people before God. As mediator, he was the only one available to approach God in the Holy of Holies. Rending his garments prohibited him from his duties.

Caiaphas was despairing over Jesus claim to be the Messiah.

In a rage of "righteous anger", he tore his garment with a theatrical display. However, his anger was far from righteous because Jesus' claim was true. By the rending of his garment, though unaware, Caiaphas symbolized the tearing away of the priesthood. For shortly thereafter, Jesus death would rend the temple's veil in two, giving access to God and nullifying the duties of earthly priests.

Notably, what Caiaphas did was a declaration of despair. In essence, the act that caused such grief was so horrible, it was beyond God's reach. Ann recognized the significance of this in the life of a believer. She acknowledged, "When we show despair in a situation, we are essentially turning our back on God and telling the people around us that He is not sufficient to see us through something."

As we know, Jesus gave us full access to God, through His death and resurrection. As Christians, we are His representatives and should convey the true nature of God's power in us. Nothing is beyond His reach. No one is out of His grasp.

"Behold, I am the Lord, the God of all flesh. Is there anything too hard for Me?" (Jeremiah 32:27 NKJV)

They asked each other, "Were not our hearts burning within us while he talked with us on the road and opened the Scriptures to us?"

Luke 24:32 (NIV)

BURNED OUT OR ABLAZE

Many things can excite a person. Just look at the average sports fan during a game. A winning goal incites cheers of elation. Good news, in general, can exhilarate us, and we can't wait to share it! A new job or promotion, a new baby or a special accomplishment are all things we can't wait to disclose.

We all have a desire to announce our triumphs. Like a candle lighting another candle, spreading the news increases the glow. The more candles lit, the brighter it is.

Imagine if you found a cure for cancer. You discovered the formula and proved its success. Would you keep it a secret? I hardly think so. Now consider that as believers we have the ultimate Good News. We have a cure for *death*.

Let's look at the Bible study of all Bible studies. Luke 24:13 starts with two disciples on the road to Emmaus. Discouraged and confused, they saw Jesus die on the cross, yet heard about an empty tomb. A stranger (Jesus) joins them on this 7-mile journey and asks what's wrong. They explain what happened. Though they believed Jesus was the Christ, they hadn't expected Him to die. They envisioned a triumphant Messiah.

Jesus explained the Old Testament passages that pointed to the Messiah. He showed them from the Scriptures that the Christ was to suffer. As Jesus opened up the Word of Truth to them, they burned with excitement. For the first time they understood God's Word regarding a suffering Savior. As the revelation sunk in, their excitement soared.

When they reached their destination, they compelled Him to stay. Hanging on every Word, they wanted to hear more. Their newfound friend agreed to join them and at the dinner table, when He broke the bread, they knew it was Jesus.

Their excitement was so great that they couldn't wait to share the good news with the disciples. In spite of it being nightfall, they returned immediately to Jerusalem.

When was the last time your heart quickened from the Word of God?

If you've been feeling burned out, let God's Word stimulate your soul. Then be ready to share!

"Because he loves me," says the
Lord, "I will rescue him;"

Psalm 91:14 (NIV)

GOD'S GOT THIS!

Pain and numbness sent Rich to the ER. His wife, Sue, stood by him when the white-coated physician entered the room, announcing, "I have bad news."

The CT showed three enlarged lymph nodes and a brain tumor. Years earlier, Rich had a melanoma removed, but now it had returned and metastasized in his lungs and brain. The diagnosis left them speechless.

"It's a tough cancer to treat," the oncologist explained. "It is incurable and will shorten your life."

For the next few days, Rich underwent scans and lab work to prepare for surgery. Battling fear, he cried out to the Lord repeatedly and each time he sensed the Lord responding that He had it. Rich felt blanketed by God's comfort, aware of his Father's voice.

On the day of the surgery, he felt the Lord tell him that he needed to show compassion to his son. A few months prior, they had a falling out. Now he hoped his son would visit.

Two days after surgery, Rich became more alert. "He'll be dead in two years," he heard a nurse say. An excruciating headache set in as they weaned him off the painkillers. Once again, he cried out to the Lord in distress, wondering why his son wasn't there. He was reassured afresh with the sense that God's got this!

The following day, Rich wanted to go home. He would need to walk the hall and climb a flight of stairs. When the time came, he felt the Lord lifting him up. To God's glory, they released him later that day.

In the first week of recovery at home, Rich struggled with pain, exhaustion, and his son's absence. In spite of a nagging depression, he experienced a stirring gratitude for his wife. As he thanked God for his blessings, he felt a supernatural comfort.

Persistent fatigue and a disappointment in his son, once more, compelled him to beseech the Lord. He felt God nudging him to stay patient and read Job. God's Word strengthened Rich's faith.

Today, Rich testifies to God's sovereignty in this. Not only did he reconnect with his son a few months later, but after receiving chemo treatments, to the doctors' amazement, Rich is cancer free.

Whatever your trial, God wants you to know, He's got it!

"Because the Lord was with him; and whatever he did, the Lord made it prosper."

Genesis 39:23 (NKJV)

CHAPTER 41

Did it ever occur to you that nothing has ever occurred to God? The One who knows the beginning from the end is never taken by surprise. Considering that He is always aware of what is going to happen, it makes sense that we should trust Him in all things.

The story of Jacob's son Joseph is a perfect example of trust. Genesis 37, 39 and 40 tell Joseph's story. Jacob, open about his favored son, gives him a distinctive coat of colors, rousing jealousy in the others. Additionally, his father uses him as an informant on his brothers' performance, causing resentment. Then on two different occasions, Joseph recounts a dream in which he is exalted above them all. Though prophetic, these dreams intensify the brothers' hatred toward him.

When Joseph meets his brothers in a distant place, they take the opportunity to rid themselves of him. First he is thrown into a pit. Then, when he is sold as a slave in Egypt, he becomes a pawn in Potiphar's house. Yet, the beginning of

Chapter 39 mentions the Lord five times. He was with Joseph and blessed him.

In spite of his promotion to overseer, Joseph, seduced by Potiphar's wife, is falsely accused of attempted rape when he refuses her. Though innocent, he is sent to prison. Yet again, the Lord was with him and prospered him. He's given the opportunity to meet the Pharaoh's chief butler and baker. When he interpreted the butler's dream, he must have thought freedom was right around the corner. But the last verse of Chapter 40 says, *"Yet the chief butler did not remember Joseph, but forgot him."* (Genesis 40:23 NKJV)

For thirteen years, Joseph is tried and tested, but the Bible records no complaints from him. It only reveals a young man willing to stand up for God and persevere in difficult circumstances. Of course, Joseph is later taken to the palace where he receives his greatest promotion. From the pit, to a pawn, to the prison, Joseph remained faithful, even though he didn't know about the palace in Chapter 41.

If you're in the midst of a trial – regardless of how long it may seem, remember - God has a Chapter 41 for you!

"But Joshua said to the people, "You cannot serve the Lord, for He is a holy God. He is a jealous God;"

Joshua 24:19 (NKJV)

COUNT THE COST

Before Joshua died, he urged the Israelites to walk in God's ways. They promised, *"Far be it from us that we should forsake the Lord to serve other gods;"* (Joshua 24:16 NKJV). They were sincere when they promised to follow God. However, Joshua told them they *couldn't* serve the Lord. He was not trying to discourage them; but simply wanted them to understand the cost of service.

Joshua knew that a full commitment to God would not be possible without God's power. He wanted the people to realize that they would only be able to follow their Lord by making Him sovereign in their lives.

In Mark 14:31, Peter made a sincere promise: *"If I have to die with You, I will not deny You!"*(NIV) and the rest of the apostles said the same. Grieved by Jesus statement that they would all stumble because of Him, they affirmed their loyalty.

Like the Israelites, they were sincere, planning to do the right thing, but not understanding the severity of the situation.

Jesus said in Luke 14:26, *"If anyone comes to Me and does not hate his father and mother, wife and children, brothers and sisters, yes, and his own life also, he cannot be My disciple,"* (NKJV)– not exactly a statement to attract disciples. Yet, Jesus wasn't looking for halfhearted followers. He wanted them to understand what devotion to Him meant.

Following Jesus is not for wimps. Many claim to be Christians but superficially live by His Word. However, Jesus made it clear that He wants fully surrendered, whole-hearted, totally devoted followers.

When we accept Jesus as Lord, we relinquish our lives to Him, giving Him all authority. "Lord" means the master who has power, authority and influence over us.

Sadly, too often, people make a commitment to "add" Jesus to their life instead of **making** Jesus their life. Jesus said, *"No one can serve two masters. Either you will hate the one and love the other, or you will be devoted to the one and despise the other."* (Matthew 6:24 NIV)

Consider God's complete dedication to you in His mercy and grace. Let it compel you to surrender your life completely to Him.

"But know that the Lord has set apart
for Himself him who is godly; The Lord
will hear when I call to Him."

Psalm 4:3 (NKJV)

ESSENTIAL EXCLUSION

Have you ever felt excluded? Maybe you weren't invited to a party, or everyone laughs at an inside joke, but you don't have a clue. At some point in our lives, we have all felt the sting of neglect.

I vividly remember being ostracized by my classmates in 6th grade. I had no friends, and though I tried to "fit in", nobody seemed interested in me. I was the shy introvert, an outcast at recess, always picked last for gym-class teams, and I ate lunch alone. Ugh!

Ultimately, exclusion hurts! We're social creatures and aloneness is not a comfortable place, for most of us. Yet, God's Word tells us that He "sets us apart" for Himself. The word "set apart" means distinguish, separate, sever. Why would God, who created us to be social, want us to be alone?

Well, first we should understand that "set apart" is NOT "set aside". God is not deserting us. He doesn't exclude us from

Himself, nor does He want us to be permanently disconnected. However, He does allow us to go through periods of separation.

Examples include Moses, whom God drove into the desert for 40 years, shaping and molding him to be a great leader. Consider King David, who ran from Saul for 10 years. Though anointed king as a teenager, God used exile to train David for the kingship he would receive at age 30. Jesus, after His baptism, spends 40 days in the wilderness alone. The apostle Paul also had a time of solitude, all part of God's refining work in his life.

Separation is a necessary part of the sanctification process. When we feel lonely, we must first accept that we are not abandoned. Satan tries to convince us of that lie, but God has a purpose in our seclusion. It may be as simple as giving us the chance to listen to Him.

If you are experiencing loneliness as a single person or a neglected spouse, or if you feel rejected by friends, family, coworkers, etc., I urge you to use this *desert time* in your life to seek God. Let Him refine you into who He wants you to be.

*"Whatever is true, whatever is noble, whatever
is right, whatever is pure, whatever is lovely,
whatever is admirable—if anything is excellent
or praiseworthy—think about such things."*

Philippians 4:8 (NIV)

GLASS HALF FULL

We've heard the analogy that an optimist sees the glass half full and the pessimist sees it half empty. Geoffrey never considered himself a pessimist. He called himself a realist, admitting that he looked at what was missing in the glass. Okay, so it is half-full, but it is also half-empty.

It's not wrong to take note of the down side of things. However, Geoffrey had a cynical attitude about everything and his life confirmed it. It was born out of a painful upbringing so it came naturally to him.

Years after Geoff became a Christian, skepticism and doubt still dominated his character. He knew the truth of the Gospel, but lacked the joy it should have brought. Then Geoff read the book of Ecclesiastes, which begins: *"Meaningless! Meaningless!" says the Teacher. "Utterly meaningless! Everything is meaningless,"* (Ecclesiastes 1:2 NIV)

At first, Geoffrey was confused. *How depressing,* he thought. King Solomon, who wrote Ecclesiastes at the end of his life, appeared to be a pessimist, like him. The book's theme is that in spite of all we do, life under the sun is meaningless. In all his magnificence, Solomon found that living apart from God was vain. Riches, power and pleasure are nothing but vanity. The book takes a sobering look at life without God. It's no surprise that the overtones are disheartening.

Geoff finished the book about Solomon's dismal view of existence and realized that without God, life *is* dismal. BUT, with God, we have the cure for pessimism. It's called faith. Faith always generates hope.

Geoff needed to increase his faith and as Romans 10:17 says, *"Faith comes by hearing, and hearing by the word of God."*(NKJV) As he studied the Bible, he understood two things about his cynicism. God hates a grumbling spirit, *"When the people complained, it displeased the Lord; … and His anger was aroused."* (Numbers 11:1 NKJV) and we are commanded to *"Do everything without complaining or arguing"* (Philippians 2:14 NIV).

Geoffrey now saw his cynical attitude as sin and confessed it. Through prayer and the Word, God changed his heart and gave him a joyful spirit that was evident to all around him.

*"If then you were raised with Christ, seek those
things which are above, where Christ is, sitting
at the right hand of God. Set your mind on
things above, not on things on the earth."*

Colossians 3:1-2 (NKJV)

SEEK THOSE THINGS ABOVE

The only people who are truly happy on earth are those whose
hearts are in heaven. Live for heaven and you'll enjoy life. How?

The first way is by living for heaven through our treasures.
Jesus said, *"Where your treasure is, there your heart will be also."*
(Matthew 6:21 NKJV) God doesn't need our money, but He
understands that we will follow after what we hold dear. Giving
back to God, raises our hearts and minds out of this temporary
world and into the eternal heaven.

Second, we live for heaven through our trials. I am convinced
that God sends us trials daily, just to keep us homesick for
heaven. If He didn't, we might become too comfortable on earth
and miss out on the work He wants to do in us. 2 Corinthians
4:16-18 states *"Therefore we do not lose heart. Even though our
outward man is perishing, yet the inward man is being renewed
day by day. For our light affliction, which is but for a moment, is*

working for us a far more exceeding and eternal weight of glory, while we do not look at the things which are seen, but at the things which are not seen. For the things which are seen are temporary, but the things which are not seen are eternal."(NKJV)

Lastly, the Lord helps us get our minds on things above through transfers – those we love who precede us to heaven. When a close family member or friend dies, or a child, even an unborn child we haven't met, we have that priceless hope of reunion waiting for us. 1 Corinthians 15:52, 54 says, *"In a moment, in the twinkling of an eye, at the last trumpet. For the trumpet will sound, and the dead will be raised incorruptible, and we shall be changed, … 'Death is swallowed up in victory.'"*(NKJV)

It may be easy to get caught up in earthly things, but God provides the solution to redirect our focus to the journey's end, *"The Rock that is higher than I,"* (Psalm 61:2 NKJV)

It's simple - seek those things above!

Contributing author: Nichole Smith

*"And Moses said to Aaron, "This is what
the Lord spoke, saying: 'By those who come
near Me I must be regarded as holy; And
before all the people I must be glorified.'"*

Leviticus 10:3 (NKJV)

HOLY HOLY

Leviticus 10 describes Nadab and Abihu offering "profane fire" to God and their subsequent death. At first glance, some may think God's swift and fatal judgement was extreme. What was so bad about their offering?

These sons of Aaron had gotten caught-up in all the excitement of the celebration. God had just sent His holy fire to consume the sacrifice and astonished the multitude into shouting and falling on their faces. Nadab and Abihu probably thought, "Hey, this is really great. Let's keep the momentum going and add some fire and incense to the altar." This carnal attitude exalted the miracle instead of the miracle Maker.

When we think we can offer God our own works on *our* own terms, we're wrong. These two brothers went ahead of God, thinking somehow they could help God out or add to what God did. It was a selfish act and shows that they did not regard God's holiness.

It was so serious that even after God's deathblow, Aaron was forbidden to openly grieve the loss of his sons. He needed to see that God's Holiness was of utmost importance and because he represented the people to God, he had to lead by example.

Today, we see a similar *profane fire* in what I like to call "spiritual hype". It is the over emphasis on emotional stimulation. Ceremonies that incite overactive worshippers into irreverent behavior. It's not wrong to sing and dance to the Lord, but there's a balance. Church services, worship meetings and the like should retain a Holy reverence to the Lord.

Preachers and worship leaders sometimes provoke a psychological commotion -"to work up what is, after all, merely a physical excitement of a strange, infectious kind, **though too often mistaken for the work of the Holy Spirit of God**." (Expositor's Bible Commentary, Fourth Series, 1890-91, Leviticus - By Rev. S. H. Kellogg, D.D., Pg. 243 *Bold type added for emphasis.*)

God is Holy! Though we may joyfully know Him as our Father, we should always possess an attitude of humility and respect. As Isaiah said after his vision of God's holiness, *"Woe is me! for I am undone;"* (Isaiah 6:5 NKJV)

*"But this I say: He who sows sparingly
will also reap sparingly, and he who sows
bountifully will also reap bountifully. So let
each one give as he purposes in his heart, not
grudgingly or of necessity; for God loves a
cheerful giver. And God is able to make all
grace abound toward you, that you, always
having all sufficiency in all things, may
have an abundance for every good work."*

2 Corinthians 9:6-8 (NKJV)

GIVING TO THE GIVER

In the early years of their marriage, Mary and Jim struggled to makes ends meet. Their finances were thin and it was hard to pay the bills. After discussing their meager circumstances, they decided that it would be best to abstain from tithing. After all, God knew they were broke. He would understand that *they* needed the money more.

Each month they took their tithe money to pay a bill. Yet, they still never had enough to keep up with their financial obligations. It was as if keeping the offering hadn't made any difference. They continued to struggle for many months until the Holy Spirit gently admonished them. Through His prompting, they felt a deep conviction to put God first. Trusting the Lord for every need meant being willing to give a portion back to Him.

Once again, they began to tithe. As they faithfully committed a portion of their income to God's service, He faithfully provided. They were blown away by His continued provision every day, week and month. Furthermore, God not only supplied the funds to pay bills, but quite often, there was money to spare.

The promise of Philippians 4:19 was affirmed in their life: *"And my God shall supply all your need according to His riches in glory by Christ Jesus."* (NKJV)

Since that lesson decades ago, Mary and Jim have persisted in regular giving, regardless of how little they may have earned. As Mary says, "God has never failed to prove all of our needs."

Giving of our resources to the work of the Lord is a privilege. *"Remembering the words the Lord Jesus himself said: 'It is more blessed to give than to receive.'"*(Acts 20:35 NIV)

If you struggle with giving, dwell on God's promises and trust Him. Then make that step of faith and see what He will do!

*"We went to the land where you sent us. It truly
flows with milk and honey, and this is its fruit.
Nevertheless the people who dwell in the land
are strong; the cities are fortified and very large;
moreover we saw the descendants of Anak there."*

Numbers 13:27-28 (NKJV)

NEVERTHELESS

Numbers 13 tells the story of those who scouted out the
Promised Land. These spies were not God's idea. Moses
recounts the story in Deuteronomy 1:21-22, *"The Lord your
God has given you the land. Go up and take possession of it …
Then all of you came to me and said, "Let us send men ahead to
spy out the land for us and bring back a report..."*(NIV)

Although God's plan did not include the spies, He allowed
it. God directed Moses to send one leader from each tribe. He
used this event to test them as they spied out the land for forty
days. Forty is the number of testing.

The result of this mission did two things. First, it proved
to the people that the land was exactly the way God described
it - fruitful and lush. Secondly, it discouraged them when they
saw the inhabitants. Interestingly, God had already told them

about those who occupied the land (Exodus 3:8). It should not have been a surprise.

Outnumbered by the ten faithless spies, Joshua and Caleb's favorable report was rejected. The people initiated the search because of unbelief and the spies amplified their doubt when they reported their fears. This resulted in the Israelites questioning God's promise.

Even though God promised them a land flowing with milk and honey, they still said, "*nevertheless,* it's not going to happen because we can't beat the enemy."

In a world filled with doubts and fears, as God's children, we should readily share our "nevertheless" reports to **encourage** faith.

> My health is failing; nevertheless, my God is sufficient. *His strength is made perfect in weakness.* (2 Cor. 12:9)

> My loved one has died; nevertheless, my God consoles me. *He is the God of all comfort.* (2 Cor. 1:3)

> My future is unsure; nevertheless, my God guides my steps. *He meets all my needs.* (Phil. 4:19)

Our circumstances may be dire; nevertheless, God's promises are true. We can say with Caleb, "*We are well able to overcome.*" (Numbers 13:30 NKJV)

"Never be lacking in zeal, but keep your spiritual fervor, serving the Lord."

Romans 12:11 (NIV)

ON FIRE

Many years ago, my husband and I were woken up in the middle of the night. Sirens blared in the midsummer's heat as smoky air wafted through the open windows. We were both tired, but the thought of something burning stirred our sense of curiosity. There had been a rash of fires locally, the work of an arson, and this one was so close. A glance outside revealed an orange glow a few blocks away.

We quickly dressed and headed outside, anticipating the sight. As expected, the scene was intense. Firefighters worked feverishly to quench the flames that engulfed an old, vacant school. My first observation, though, was the hundreds of bystanders watching the spectacle. Like us, they had all been lured from their homes in the wee hours of the morning to see the fire.

That experience makes me wonder if we could attract people similarly. Someone once said, "Get on fire for God and men will come and see you burn."

When Paul writes about spiritual fervor, the word for fervor means hot or glowing. The New Testament emphasizes that Christians remain "on fire". Jesus says of those who are *"Neither hot nor cold--I am about to spit you out of my mouth."* (Revelation 3:16 NIV) and we are compelled to *"not quench the Spirit"* in 1 Thessalonians 5:19 (NKJV).

Fire is both destructive and purifying. Jesus said, *"I have come to bring fire on the earth,"* (Luke 12:49 NIV) Believers will be proved and purified by fire which will, *"Test the quality of each person's work."* (1 Corinthians 3:13 NIV) God can use fire to refine us and to judge us.

Throughout the Bible, fire illustrates the power, holiness and judgement of God. We see it in the burning bush, the pillar of fire in the desert, and the sacrifices consumed by flames. John the Baptist said of Jesus, *"He will baptize you with the Holy Spirit and fire,"* (Matt 3:11b NIV), so we can see that it is essential to our walk.

If you are growing cold in your spiritual walk, make the decision to rekindle your devotion to the Lord. Feed the flames with the Word of God. Fan the flames with prayer.

A passion for God is sure to attract attention!

"Then he said to them all:
"Whoever wants to be my disciple must deny themselves
and take up their cross daily and follow me."

Luke 9:23 (NIV)

RENOVATION OR ANIHILATION

As Christians, we tend to think fondly of the cross, knowing it is the symbol of salvation. We may ponder more deeply the suffering Savior when we take communion or hear the Passion story. For the most part, a cross is something we happily identify with, often wearing them on our jewelry or t-shirts, hanging them on our walls or putting stickers of them on our vehicles.

It's true that the cross represents who we are in Christ. But, when Jesus says *"Whoever does not take up their cross and follow me is not worthy of me"* (Matthew 10:38 NIV), He is declaring a serious ultimatum.

Taking up our cross means "death". The cross was an instrument of execution, not a pretty picture! Jesus wasn't trivializing the cross. In fact, He was signifying the gravity of what it means to follow Him.

When we accept Christ as our Savior, we have chosen the way of the cross. We have chosen death to this life in exchange for eternal life. As Galatians 2:20 states; *"I have been crucified with Christ <u>and I no longer live</u>, but Christ lives in me."* (NIV Emphasis added) Of course, our physical lives don't end when we receive salvation, but in a spiritual sense, we have put our "old self" to death.

"Therefore, if anyone is in Christ, he is a new creation; old things have passed away; behold, all things have become new." (2 Corinthians 5:17 NKJV) God looks at us not wanting to renovate, but instead decides to rebuild from scratch! The old must be annihilated before He can do the work.

Unfortunately, we are inclined to pick up our dead body, wanting to do something good. These "works of the flesh" reek with the repulsive stench of a rotting corpse. They are as useless as a carcass and with them we cannot hope to please God.

The apostle Paul said, *"For I know that in me (that is, in my flesh) nothing good dwells;"* (Romans 7:18 NKJV) When we accept that truth, we allow God to work in us. Let us daily ask God to reveal to us our deeds, either as a sweet fragrance or foul odor.

*"Saul, Saul, why are you persecuting me? It
is hard for you to kick against the goads."*

Acts 26:14b (NKJV)

AGAINST THE WIND

Going against God's plan can make life frustrating. Ron found that out the hard way when he agreed to partner in business with an unbeliever. He didn't want to admit he had made a mistake.

Before making the commitment, he talked with his pastor, who counseled him against it, quoting 2 Corinthians 6:14: *"Do not be unequally yoked with unbelievers. For what partnership has righteousness with lawlessness?"* (NKJV) However, Ron felt he could win his business partner to Christ and looked at it as an opportunity for both his company and evangelism.

During the weeks and months following his merger, Ron found himself missing church and ministry commitments. The new business venture was a burden that was taking its toll on his spiritual life. In addition, his business partner refused to see his perspective on financial integrity, which weighed heavy on him.

On a rare Sunday morning visit to church, Ron listened to a

sermon on the Apostle Paul's conversion. He thought carefully about the Lord's words to Paul, *"It's hard for you to kick against the goads."* (Acts 26:14b NKJV) As the pastor explained the verse, Ron sensed the Holy Spirit speaking to him, but he tried to ignore it.

When he got home, he planned to clear the backyard of the fallen leaves, capitalizing on his free time and the sunny weather. Taking the leaf blower, Ron began his task. He started at one corner of the yard, blowing the leaves into a pile. As he compassed the mound, a sudden gust of wind scattered the leaves, undoing his work.

Frustrated, Ron tried to work faster, corralling the leaves the best he could. However, as soon as he made headway, another gust unraveled his progress. When his frustration turned to anger, he barked out a prayer, "Really, God? Could you please help me here?"

Despite the loud humming of the leaf blower, Ron heard the gentle whisper from the Lord, asking him why he was fighting against the wind. He stopped, shut off the blower, and sank to his knees.

Surrounded by the orange and red hues of autumn, Ron got right with God. He saw clearly that God had been calling him out of the partnership. The stinging goad had prodded his conscience to obedience.

*"Cast your cares on the Lord
and he will sustain you;"*

Psalm 55:22 (NIV)

SWEET SURRENDER

The story of Hannah in 1 Samuel shows how God uses circumstances to bring about His purposes. God wanted to change the poor state of Israel and needed a woman who would train her child to honor Him and be able to give that child up to the Lord's service.

The struggle wasn't just her desire for a child, but the stigma attached to being barren. She probably believed she would eventually get pregnant, thinking God was teaching her patience. However, after years of infertility, she would start getting the "look" from family members. Their brows furrowed in silent accusation; suspecting some secret sin in her life.

I imagine her praying; "Lord, why would you allow this? I've been obedient to your commands. I'm submissive to Elkanah. I don't retaliate to Peninnah's taunting accusations. I want to trust, but every month I see the blood stain that tells me, 'No'. It's become a cycle of incrimination. Every time I hear a baby cry, my heart sinks. Can it plunge any deeper? My neighbor is expecting again. As they celebrate the news, I feel like I'm drowning. Peninnah is delighted, eyeing me as though she won some spiteful match. Even Elkanah can't make up for the hurt, though I know it hurts him, too. I wonder, is he questioning my barrenness? He doesn't encourage me anymore. Has he given up, Lord? Is he beginning to see judgement in place of testing?"

Hannah was a righteous woman, and shouldering the weight of a misconceived shame was unbearable.

In her anguish, she thought if she had one son, it would prove to everyone that she wasn't under God's judgment. If God would allow it, she would gladly give him right back. She would raise him as a Nazirite and dedicate his life to the Lord's service. She would bring him to the tabernacle at age five. Naturally, that would mean she would only see him occasionally, but she could live with that.

When Hannah was willing to surrender the one thing she most wanted, God was able to do the one thing she most needed. Her sacrifice allowed God to change a nation through Samuel, and in the end, He blessed Hannah with five more children.

"No temptation has overtaken you except what is common to mankind. And God is faithful; he will not let you be tempted beyond what you can bear. But when you are tempted, he will also provide a way out so that you can endure it."

1 Corinthians 10:13 (NIV)

ONE QUESTION, TWO HEARTS

It was the 5th Annual "Skip Day" for Rich's company. Designed to reward employees with a paid day-off, the event offered food and fun at a local entertainment venue.

Upon arrival, Rich noticed some coworkers already drinking, as this was a social event and the company permitted it. As a believer, he wanted to be a light in this place, but the atmosphere seemed awkward for a witnessing opportunity. Yet, he knew his own actions would have their influence and he determined to show the light of Christ by example.

As the day moved on, while Rich was bowling, he overheard a coworker who had had too much to drink. The man was watching TV and making crude remarks about the female entertainer on the screen.

Rich felt prompted to say something. "Would you marry her?" he asked.

With a stunned expression, the man responded, "No!"

Without another word, Rich noticed that his coworker's demeanor changed. He began to settle down. There was a visible change in his thought process. Undoubtedly, the Holy Spirit had prompted that remark.

A little later, Rich heard the voice of temptation as he looked around the room at a number of attractive women. *I should have no problem getting to know any of these women* the thought came to him. As swiftly as the tempter's invitation came, the Spirit gave a gentle reminder. Rich asked himself, *Would I marry her?*

He smiled as he recognized the Lord's interception. Rich marveled at how God used the previous incident to evoke a proper response. The very question he asked his coworker was exactly what he needed to hear.

Rich departed the event, reminded that being bound to Christ meant being separate from the world. He considered the burden of temptations and the condemnation that comes when the line of sin is crossed.

To Rich's amazement, the message at Bible Study that evening was about the very same thing. God promises to help us when we're tempted, but if we fail, His grace brings forgiveness.

*"You, dear children, are from God and have
overcome them, because the one who is in you
is greater than the one who is in the world."*

1 John 4:4 (NIV)

WEAK WEAPONRY

Late in the evening, on a dark city street, a man walks home
alone, cautious of his surroundings. Suddenly, a figure appears
from an alleyway! A menacing voice demands his wallet. At
first, the man contemplates putting up a fight, but the thief
dispels that idea by revealing a large blade. Tightly clenching
his weapon, the attacker repeats his demand, "Hand over your
wallet!" The unarmed victim is no match for this foe. Helplessly,
he relinquishes his wallet.

Unfortunately, the man was unaware of one very important
fact. His attacker was wielding a rubber knife. Had he known,
he could easily have overcome the scrawny thug. Instead, he
was robbed of his money, his credit cards and his personal
information.

Like the victim in this story, Christians sometimes surrender
to their enemy, giving up their precious valuables. Jesus said in
John 10:10, *"The thief comes only to steal and kill and destroy".*

(NIV) Our enemy wants to steal our joy, kill our faith, and destroy our ministry, and he succeeds often enough. But why?

Colossians 2:15 says that Jesus, *"disarmed the powers and authorities,"* (NIV) on the cross. So ultimately, Satan has no power over us, **unless** we give it to him. *"For though we live in the world, we do not wage war as the world does. The weapons we fight with are not the weapons of the world. On the contrary, they have divine power to demolish strongholds. We demolish arguments and every pretension that sets itself up against the knowledge of God, and we take captive every thought to make it obedient to Christ."* (2 Corinthians 10:3-5 NIV)

Sometimes we think Satan has power to hurt us, but, in reality, his weapons are impotent. He may taunt us with fear, discouragement, indifference, and unbelief, but we don't need to succumb to them. Satan's tactics aim to take our eyes off Jesus, weakening us. With a misplaced focus, we become an easy target.

If you're feeling like Satan's prey, brandish the powerful "Sword of the Spirit" which says, *"Submit yourselves, then, to God. Resist the devil, and he will flee from you."* (James 4:7 NIV)

"Beloved, do not think it strange concerning the fiery trial which is to try you, as though some strange thing happened to you;"

1 Peter 4:12 (NKJV)

YOLO

The storm blows in as unexpected news from your doctor, your boss, your spouse… Whether it's a health crisis, financial downpour or squall in a relationship, suffering will come to us. They can be as minor as an inconvenience, or as extreme as a tragedy, and we learn to cope with them in different ways.

Often, people find ways of bypassing the pain and anguish with distraction. Some try to outweigh their grief with pleasure, so that at the end of the day, the greater impression is good. Pleasure becomes a diversion, which helps numb the effects of adversity.

Those who seek this kind of reprieve may hold to the YOLO or the "You Only Live Once" philosophy. However, this way of thinking will not necessarily better us. It only serves to get us through the trial until the next one comes.

As believers, we are told in 1 Peter that tribulations are present to try us. *"In all this you greatly rejoice, though now for a little while you may have had to suffer grief in all kinds of trials. These have come so that the proven genuineness of your faith—of greater worth than gold, which perishes even though refined by fire—may result in praise, glory and honor when Jesus Christ is revealed."* (1 Peter 1:6-7 NIV)

Suffering is part of life, so there should be no surprise when trials come. We may not know the reason, but God has a purpose in our suffering, using it in His greater plan.

When we suffer, it doesn't mean that God is picking on us. He doesn't take pleasure in it, and He doesn't cause it. He just uses it to bring us closer to Him. James 1:13 says, *"When tempted, no one should say, 'God is tempting me.' For God cannot be tempted by evil, nor does he tempt anyone;"* in verse 12, James encourages us with, *"Blessed is the one who perseveres under trial because, having stood the test, that person will receive the crown of life that the Lord has promised to those who love him."*(NIV)

Trials are part of the sanctification process. Welcome its transforming presence.

"For you were once darkness, but now you are light in the Lord. Live as children of light."

Ephesians 5:8 (NIV)

A WALK IN THE DARK

Have you ever walked through a dark room? Maybe the power was out, or you didn't feel like turning on a light. The latter scenario happened to me. I knew the room well and thought I could cross to the exit on the other side. I'd done it hundreds of times in the light, so why not trust my instincts? All would have been well, except for a misplaced chair in my path.

The resulting pain in my knee taught me an important lesson - darkness hides obstacles, and I should never assume the path is clear.

Light is a blessing. With it, we can avoid the obstacles and the consequences that arise from a collision. Light, even at its dimmest, aids our walk.

In the spiritual realm, we are called to walk in the light. *"O house of Jacob, come and let us walk in the light of the Lord."* (Isaiah 2:5 NKJV)

God wants to see His children succeed. He knows that if we walk in darkness, we will stumble. Simply put, if I had turned on a light, I would have seen the chair and navigated around it with ease. So too, when we walk in God's light, we have a clearer picture of things that hinder our growth.

So, how do we "walk in the light" spiritually? Jesus gave us the answer when He said, *"I am the light of the world. He who follows Me shall not walk in darkness, but have the light of life."* (John 8:12 NKJV)

Walking is a forward motion showing progress and maturity. It is no different spiritually, and we have a spiritual flashlight – God's Word. *"Your word is a lamp for my feet, a light on my path."* (Psalm 119:105 NIV) As we seek God through the light of His Word, we can clearly see His path. The obstructions of sin and other distractions are in plain view, making it easy to avoid them.

Furthermore, by walking in the light, we have a glow about us that attracts those in darkness. As "children of light", we reflect Jesus in our lives. Therefore, I encourage you to mature in Christ and *"Let your light shine before others."* (Matthew 5:16 NIV)

"Clothe yourselves with compassion, kindness,
humility, gentleness and patience. Bear with
each other and forgive one another if any of you
has a grievance against someone. Forgive as the
Lord forgave you. But above all these things
put on love, which is the bond of perfection."

Colossians 3:12-14 (NIV)

ADMIRABLE ATTIRE

In this day and age, the word "love" is tossed around carelessly, and is often used by those having illicit relations. In fact, we use the term "lovers" to describe couples in adultery and "making love" to describe sex. What is love, really?

The Bible has a lot to say about love. To mention a few, Luke 6:35 tells us to love our enemies. Mark 12:30-31 gives us the two greatest commandments; love the Lord with all our heart, and love our neighbor as ourselves. 1 Corinthians 13:13 says that out of faith, hope and love, love is the greatest. 1 Peter 4:8 informs us that love covers a multitude of sin. 1 John 4:18 teaches that perfect love casts out fear.

Obviously, love is more than an emotion. The world's

definition of love is very different from what God intended. As children of God, we should be examples of true love.

Paul tells us to wear love like a garment, comprised of *"compassion, kindness, humility, gentleness and patience."* (Colossians 3:12 NIV) He adds that *above all* we must put on "love", which he calls the bond of perfection. The word bond in the Greek is *"sundesmos"*, which comprises the words *sun* meaning "close union" and *desmos*, which means "shackle (as for a prisoner)". Love holds us together!

Paul equates love to a band that secures the rest of the garment. It reminds me of the time I attended a party as a young teenager. Wearing a gown that belonged to my older sister, I found myself struggling all night. The dress, two sizes too big, hindered my movement with its lengthy skirt and worried me as I tried to keep it from falling off my shoulders. It was a miserable evening.

Without love, our acts of compassion, kindness and so on, are cumbersome and awkward. We can be easily tripped up and have a disheveled appearance.

As you contemplate your actions of love, ask God to give you a glimpse of your heart and see how you're dressed.

*"Blessed is the one ...whose delight is in
the law of the Lord, and who meditates on
his law day and night. That person is like
a tree planted by streams of water, which
yields its fruit in season and whose leaf does
not wither—whatever they do prospers."*

Psalm 1:1-3 (NIV)

LESSONS FROM A LITTLE ONE

Samantha was a young mom and feeling overwhelmed at times. Some days, it seemed like the responsibility of motherhood and keeping house consumed her time. One afternoon, after putting a roast in the oven, she was looking forward to spending some quality time with her toddler.

Samantha sat with her son on the floor in the nursery, but two-year-old Kyle had different plans. He made several attempts at leaving his room, so Samantha closed the door, hoping the toys she held would appeal to him. However, Kyle was not interested.

She tried her best to delight her little boy, but, sadly, his focus was the closed door. He leaned on it, whining for his freedom. Samantha sighed. She just wanted to spend time with him. *I wish you understood how much joy we could share together.*

As those words formed in her mind, there was no doubt they came from God. But He was speaking them to **her**. *Have I been so preoccupied?* she wondered, and then considered her own focus lately. Being a young mother required a lot of her time and energy, yet God was showing her that the greatest strength comes from spending time with Him.

When we are self-absorbed with our own desires, we fail to recognize the preciousness of time spent with our heavenly Father. As Samantha learned, from time to time God will close doors in our lives, prompting us to commune with Him.

A willful attitude blinds us to the blessings God has in store and, like a stubborn two-year-old, we become miserable and discontent.

If you find yourself "whining" and unhappy, the remedy is simple:

Remember who you are in Christ, *"See what great love the Father has lavished on us, that we should be called children of God! And that is what we are!"* (1 John 3:1 NIV)

Then spend time with Him. When you do, He promises intimacy: *"Come near to God and he will come near to you."* (James 4:8 NIV)

*"So do not fear, for I am with you; do not
be dismayed, for I am your God. I will
strengthen you and help you; I will uphold
you with my righteous right hand"*

Isaiah 41:10 (NIV)

HIS MIGHTY RIGHT HAND

It was at the closing of a women's retreat, during worship, when I heard those words from Isaiah. Verse 13 continued, *"For I am the LORD your God who takes hold of your right hand and says to you, Do not fear; I will help you"*. (Isaiah 41:13 NIV)

It was just a moment, in a string of verses read over us, but for some reason (a God-reason), it struck me. The imagery of it was so powerful, so clear. The righteous right hand of God will uphold me. He will lift me up when I am dismayed.

In my mind, I could see His mighty right hand reaching down from heaven. As I sang, I lifted my own right hand, stretching towards Him, trusting that He could give me strength in my journey, no matter what the circumstance. I felt physically lighter, filled with an emotional and spiritual lucidity I'd never experienced before.

Later, when reading the Bible, I found this reference of

God lifting us with His right hand repeated several times. This was significant, not just because I felt moved by the verses, but because of the numerous times it's mentioned.

During my research, I found 58 Bible verses using the phrase "the right hand of God" signifying power and authority. It's why Jesus sits at the right hand of the Father, as one holding power and authority over everything.

Yet, there is another fascinating piece to this. Though I'm no scholar, I wonder if there's not something deeply significant about the fact that God lifts us – His creation – with His right hand. The fact is He loves us so radically, so deeply, and so thoroughly. He strengthens us and brings us up with His mighty right hand, to redeem us and set us apart as His own children.

Often now, when I worship, I think of this significance and raise my hand, thanking God for His total and complete love for us; that even while I am in my imperfect human state, He would reach down with His powerful right hand and uphold me.

Contributing author: Christina Hicks

"Peace I leave with you,…"

John 14:27 (NKJV)

INEXPLICABLE PEACE

Dick prepared to fly to Dallas, where he would make an important presentation. Though it was an honor, he was nervous. Moments before heading to the airport, the phone rang. He learned that his mother had cancer and had only three months to live.

This grim news made the trip agonizing. Upon arrival, with his presentation scheduled for the next day and his mom's prognosis looming, Dick's anxiety spiraled out of control.

He planned to meet some associates for dinner, but knew he needed time in prayer to calm his nerves. Alone in his hotel room, Dick battled his fear and uncertainty on his knees.

He prayed for peace and wisdom concerning his mom's illness. He also asked God to grant her wish to live five more years. He continued fervently praying, unaware of the time. He checked his watch; four hours had passed, it was 9 p.m. Too late for dinner, he had a quick snack, and went to bed.

The next morning, Dick had an inexplicable peace. He was

excited to give his presentation and the meeting was a complete success.

Later at the hotel, Dick entered an elevator with a group of people. The last to get on was an older woman carrying a section of newspaper. After ascending numerous floors, the elevator jolted and began to plunge. Only Dick and the woman were calm. Everyone else screamed in terror.

The elevator car abruptly stopped. Then came the deafening boom of elevator cables crashing above them. The frantic passengers continued to shriek.

Dick's unexplainable peace allowed him to call for help and alleviate some of the tension with a few jokes. As the fire department worked on their rescue, Dick's humor helped the passengers relax.

Three hours later, they exited one at a time. Of the two who remained, the woman handed Dick the newspaper and told him to read it. As she exited, Dick opened the paper. Astounded, he read; *"What You Need to Know About Dealing with Cancer"*. How could she have possibly known? He rushed off the elevator but couldn't find her in the crowd of people. He never saw her again.

Unquestionably, God was at work, and by His grace, Dick's mom lived another five years!

"Truly I tell you," Jesus replied, "no one who has left home or brothers or sisters or mother or father or children or fields for me and the gospel will fail to receive a hundred times as much in this present age: homes, brothers, sisters, mothers, children and fields—along with persecutions—and in the age to come eternal life."

Mark 10:29-30 (NIV Emphasis added)

DID YOU SAY PERSECUTIONS?

Did you ever read a contract and then balk at the fine print, or notice the tiny text disclaimers on products? Some labels are warnings, like the car sunshade that cautions users to "Remove from windshield before driving", or the peanut container that warns, "This product may contain peanuts," or the child's Superman costume that alerts, "Wearing of this garment does not enable you to fly."

However, not all waivers are silly. For the few who actually read such statements, the information can be eye-opening. Claims may reveal outrageous interest rates, unfair expectations of the buyer, or complete limitation of liability for the seller, to name a few.

Advertisers and marketing agents have learned the art of impunity through disclaimers, freeing companies from responsibility and accountability. These clauses are typically contained in four-point font or in audio form as rapid-fire statements that are barely coherent.

Unlike the world, Jesus never made false promises nor did He try to hide the hard truth. The Bible is replete with statements about persecution. In fact, Jesus *promised* it. All four Gospels state that the world will hate us because of our relationship to Christ. (Matthew 10:22, Mark 13:13, Luke 21:17, John 15:19)

Similar to the doctor that says, "This won't hurt a bit," right before giving a painful injection; concealing the harsh truth is wrong. Even if it's hard to swallow, our preparedness depends on it.

Jesus gave full-disclosure to all those who would follow Him. Numerous times, He warned His disciples of the suffering they would bear on His account. Yet, they never seemed to hear Him. Often, like the disciples, we downplay the warnings, especially when witnessing. After all, no one wants to hear that persecution is "part of the deal".

However, Jesus' warning comes with another incredible promise. *"I have told you these things, so that in me you may have peace. In this world you will have trouble. But take heart! I have overcome the world."* (John 16:33 NIV)

*"Rejoice inasmuch as you participate in
the sufferings of Christ, so that you may be
overjoyed when his glory is revealed;"*

1 Peter 4:13 (NIV)

GOD'S DISPLAY

One day, I was doing yardwork and listening to worship music. Being in the midst of a trial, I was keenly aware that God was working on my heart. As I meditated on a particular worship song, a clear but remote thought came to me, as if outside myself: Would I be willing to suffer through a trial, knowing it was meant to affect someone else?

At first, I wondered if the thought came from my own head. I had never considered my trials were exclusively for someone else. As I pondered it a little more, I knew that God was prompting me to consider that trials are not always about the person suffering.

I remembered the blind man that Jesus healed. Because he was born blind, the disciples wanted to know if it was his sin or his parents' sin that caused the malady. Jesus said, *"Neither,"* but that *"This happened so that the works of God might be displayed in him."* (John 9:3 NIV)

In the passage, he is called a **man** so he must have been at least twenty, and he remained blind his entire life to that point. Yet, God allowed him to suffer this ailment in order to receive glory. His blindness had meaning.

I thought about the question again. Would I be willing to go through a trial, so the works of God could be displayed in me? As a showcase of God's works, my suffering would affect *others*.

God allows afflictions for many reasons. I can attest to personally growing because of the trials that I've been through. But, I hadn't considered that a trial I had endured, may be for someone else's edification.

Sin is the ultimate cause of suffering, but it is part of God's plan to conform His mercy towards an afflicted humankind, permitting hardship and adversity. By this, He teaches us to cherish His blessings and hold dear His grace that unites us ever closer to Him.

I considered my answer to the question. If God sees my suffering as an opportunity to bring glory to Himself, how can I say "No"?

"May your will be done, Lord."

"Behold, I have refined you, but not as silver; I have tested you in the furnace of affliction. For My own sake, for My own sake, I will do it;"

Isaiah 48:10-11 (NKJV)

FAITHFUL FILTER

My severe allergy to rabbits meant that Cocoa, our new brown cottontail, would need to live in a rabbit hutch outside. It was spring, and he managed well for the next few seasons. However, when fall turned to winter, threatened with bitter cold temperatures, we decided to bring Cocoa into the garage below the house.

One particularly cold night, I woke up, struggling for air, as if I was breathing through a straw. I had an inhaler for emergencies and used it immediately. Within minutes, the medicine opened up my airways. I could breathe normally again.

The next morning, we tried to determine the cause of my bronchial attack. We figured it had to be Cocoa. But how did his dander reach my lungs? My husband realized that the freezing temperatures caused the heat to come on in the garage.

As a forced hot air system, the furnace carried air from the garage all through the house.

Not wanting pipes to freeze, the garage would need to remain heated, but Cocoa would not survive outside. Our dilemma resolved with a trip to the home improvement store and the purchase of a hypoallergenic furnace filter. The old filter allowed Cocoa's dander to pass through the system.

When it comes to trials, God's hand is like a filter. He doesn't prevent all the evil in the world from affecting us, but He does sift it through his divine wisdom.

Often, we think that if God loves us, He wouldn't allow us harm. Yet, sometimes, pain is essential for our greater good. Like the sting of the vaccination needle in your child's arm, trials are painful, but necessary.

Additionally, God takes our pain and recycles it for the greater good beyond ourselves. When we struggle through a trial and emerge victoriously, we gain a new compassion for others who go through similar ordeals, giving us a unique ability to minister. We can be assured that our pain is beneficial and also has a purpose!

God refines us for His own sake. No matter what hardship we endure, God has sifted it through His sovereign filter.

"In him and through faith in him we may
approach God with freedom and confidence."

Ephesians 3:12 (NIV)

ALL ACCESS PASS

Garrett's friend knew a guy. "A friend of the drummer," he said. That's how they got a hold of the VIP tickets. It would be the concert of the year, maybe even the decade. The band was legendary and Garrett had all their albums. Going to the event was exciting enough, but when his coworker mentioned VIP tickets, he practically flipped. VIP tickets meant a backstage pass, and that would be the thrill of a lifetime. He could hardly contain himself. Would he actually get to meet the members of the band?

Garrett's all-access pass allowed him to go where few were permitted. He got to see the band up close during their performance, got to meet them personally with a small group of VIP ticket-holders, and even got to tour their dressing room. It was truly memorable.

However, in spite of this great opportunity, Garrett walked away no different. Though impressive, it was not a life changing experience. It wasn't until he met Jesus years later that the memory of the concert spoke to him.

Garrett had been dealing with guilt. After a few years with the Lord, he had experienced his first big spiritual failure. Though he believed God had forgiven him, he still felt unworthy to pray. Then he read Hebrews 10:19-20, 22: *"Since we have confidence to enter the Most Holy Place by the blood of Jesus, by a new and living way opened for us through the curtain, that is, his body... let us draw near to God with a sincere heart and with the full assurance that faith brings."*(NIV) Garrett understood. Jesus death tore the veil to the Holy of Holies. He made it possible for us to approach God the Father through the Son.

He remembered the VIP privilege he had where he was able to go into a restricted area. Had he said, "No, I'll just stay with the crowd, here in row 28. I'm sure the concert will be fine from back here," his friend would have called him crazy. He dropped to his knees, entered the throne room and felt God's transforming power.

Jesus is our "all-access" pass. Nothing should hold us back from approaching our heavenly Father.

"Let us acknowledge the Lord; let us press on to acknowledge him. As surely as the sun rises, he will appear; he will come to us like the winter rains, like the spring rains that water the earth.""

Hosea 6:3 (NIV)

INTIMATE GOD

For some people, "intimate" and "God" are opposites. Intimate, meaning up close and personal and God the Almighty Creator of the universe, who, by definition would seem inapproachable. However, for the follower of Christ, God's intimacy is the motivating element to faith. He is a blessed paradox of holiness and intimacy.

Today's world bombards us with distraction. Noise is prevalent. Visual stimulation is over the top. Peace and quiet are practically extinct. With such preoccupation, Christians are becoming less and less apt to find intimacy with God.

While staying at a cabin in the mountains, my husband and I looked forward to a picturesque evening. We decided that a glowing fire in the fireplace would be the finishing touch. After arranging the logs and igniting the tinder, the flames began to leap. It wasn't long before the dry wood was ablaze. It would have been a perfect night, but as the fire died down, the room began to fill up with smoke.

The problem was a loss of draft. As the heat from the flames rise, the chimney draws smoke up and out of the room. Because the cabin windows were closed, the pressure in the room decreased as the fire burned. When the pressure was too low, the fire began to die down and air came back through the chimney, bringing smoke with it. Once we opened some windows and stoked the fire, the room began to clear. However, our peaceful evening became unpleasant and I went to bed smelling like soot.

I learned an important lesson about fireplace mechanics that night, but more than that, God showed me how important it is for us to rekindle the fire of intimacy with Him. When we forget to open up the windows of prayer and devotional time, we choke our spiritual fire. As the flames diminish, an influx of smoky distractions smother us, making it hard to breathe or see, and ultimately making us stink.

How do we keep the flames going? Getting to know God. Read Ephesians 1:15-23. It is my prayer for you!

"For it is by grace you have been saved, through faith—and this is not from yourselves, it is the gift of God— not by works, so that no one can boast."

Ephesians 2:8-9 (NIV)

NO STRINGS ATTACHED

Jerry was convinced. This was a bargain. How could he pass it up? But his wife's protruding stare kept him from giving the final "okay". The salesman smiled, believing he'd closed the deal he extended his clipboard and said "You can sign right here."

"Could I have a minute with my wife?" Jerry finally replied. The salesman furrowed his brow and nodded.

"What's wrong?" Jerry pleaded. "Didn't you hear what he said?" his wife implored.

"We can afford the monthly payment," he defended, "And they're being very generous with the upgrades. We'll never get another deal like this."

Calmly, his wife opened the calculator app on her phone and started punching in numbers. Jerry smiled at the agent and gestured with his index finger then turned to her, "He's waiting."

Without a word, she turned the phone to her husband. "Forty-five thousand?" he inquired, reading the number back to her. "Is that vehicle worth forty-five thousand dollars?" she asked casually. "Forty-five? Really?" Jerry stammered.

His wife showed him the breakdown of the lease agreement. "When three years are up, that's how much you'll have paid with the buyout." The realization hit hard and Jerry's excitement waned. The lease was not a good idea. Jerry was sorry he wouldn't be driving away in a nice new car, but he was happy he had avoided a financial blow.

Many "deals" in this world are too good to be true. Thousands of people are cheated out of their hard-earned money because they don't read the fine print or are simply unaware of the hidden fees, high interest rates, and erroneous charges. This leads people to be skeptical, and understandably so.

Unfortunately, when it comes to salvation, some people dispute the idea that God would offer it freely. They find it easier to believe that God expects us to work for heaven. Many religions stem from this understanding, teaching a work-based faith.

Truthfully, there is a high price for salvation. But Jesus already paid it. Now, out of His great love for us, He offers it freely. We only need to accept it.

"Come and see the works of God; He is awesome in His doing toward the sons of men."

Psalm 66:5 (NKJV)

AWESOME GOD

From birth, Joanne endured a defect that caused her left eye to turn inward. She wished the flaw would go away, and even prayed for healing, but when nothing changed, she resolved to accept the way God made her.

Decades passed, and she was attending a Sunday night prayer service at her church. Toward the end of the evening, the pastor called the elders forward to anoint people for healing. Joanne went to the front of the sanctuary, intending to ask for prayer for a sore shoulder. However, while waiting in line, she sensed an unmistakable prompt to ask for prayer for her eye.

Her first response was to protest; *No way!* she resisted. Then, as her heart began to pound, she argued; *It would be foolish of me to bring that up.* Now perspiring, she began to negotiate; *I will only do this if the pastor is available.* She felt more comfortable sharing this request with the pastor and she knew she could back out if he wasn't available when it was her turn.

As the line moved forward, her opportunity arrived. Lo and

behold, the pastor was open for her. She approached him and gave in to the prompting. He prayed for her eye and she went back to her seat, doubtful and disappointed. But, over the next few days, she forgot all about it.

Weeks later, Joanne finished a search for a new optometrist. She and her husband had recently moved and she needed to replace all her doctors locally. On that first visit, the eye doctor asked her if she had ever considered having her left eye straightened. Amazed at the question, Joanne replied that she didn't know it was possible. Soon after, she saw an ophthalmologist who informed her of a very successful treatment.

Joanne had the procedure done and her eye recovered with perfect alignment. Only then did she remember that night of prayer. The Holy Spirit moved her to pray and in spite of her doubts and fears, God still worked this miracle. All along, God intended to bring healing to her. Captivated by His love, she stands in awe of her awesome God!

"We speak as those approved by God to be entrusted with the gospel. We are not trying to please people but God, who tests our hearts."

1 Thessalonians 2:4 (NIV)

MAGNIFICENT OBSCURITY

The predominant record of Jesus earthly life is from His last three years. The Bible is mostly silent about His childhood. The Scriptures tell of His birth, give insight to His being about His Father's business at age twelve and clarify that He grew in stature, wisdom and favor with God and men.

Most of what Jesus did for his first thirty years is unknown. Yet, that silence rings loud in a magnificent way.

His parents knew He was special. When presenting Jesus at the temple as a baby, two worshippers came and honored Him, knowing He was the Messiah. Mary, in particular, must have wondered when He would "do something" befitting His glory.

We know He had brothers and sisters, and was likely a carpenter, as it was customary for the son to follow in the trade of his father. Family life would have been very ordinary. "So what?" you may ask. The fact that God Almighty, in a human body, spent time as a typical boy, teenager, and man says a lot.

Jesus, with all His ability, with all His wisdom and power, remained ordinary. He didn't readily cure diseases, didn't prevent injuries or whip up miracles to remedy the problems of the day. Had He done this early on, surely His family and friends would not have doubted His ministry. Instead, they thought He was insane. *"When his family heard about this, they went to take charge of him, for they said, "He is out of his mind."* (Mark 3:21 NIV)

The fact is that Jesus lived as one of us, without popularity, an unknown until He was thirty years old. At the wedding in Cana, wanting to remain obscure, He told His mother His hour had "not yet come." Despite His ability to perform miracles, He was content to simply be human.

By remaining obscure, Jesus could experience humanity.

This can be a great lesson to us in that, if Jesus in all His magnificence was content to be ordinary, we too should be content to live in obscurity, desiring recognition from God.

Are you living for the accolades of men?

*"Just as people are destined to die once,
and after that to face judgment, so Christ
was sacrificed once to take away the sins of
many; and he will appear a second time,
not to bear sin, but to bring salvation
to those who are waiting for him."*

Hebrews 9:27-28 (NIV)

MERCIFUL CANCER

Those two words seem contradictory, but consider this:

It is an image many will not forget. A TV reporter, calmly interviewing a woman when suddenly gunshots ring out. Brief images of terror and harrowing screams are cut short and a confused anchorman fumbles for words. Two people, killed in a moment's time, leaving the nation in shock. The first thought that came to me was, "Were they ready?"

Whether by the hands of a murderer or an unforeseen accident, death comes to many without warning. However, what if we had a timeframe for death? What if we were given notice? For some people, cancer is that notice.

Terminal illness can be a gift. That may sound insensitive, but consider these points. Everyone dies. That is a fact. There is no guarantee of reaching old age. The Bible says, *"All the days ordained for me were written in your book before one of them came to be."* (Psalm 139:16 NIV)

God knows our final day, even if we don't. Yet, when we face a diagnosis like cancer, we are bound to contemplate our mortality.

For the unbeliever, it can be the catalyst of surrendering to God. By far, this is the best thing that can happen to someone who may go on to lose his physical life, but will then attain eternal life. For the Christian, such a diagnosis can strengthen our faith and deepen our relationship with God, ultimately providing a witness to those around us.

My diagnosis of leukemia gave me an entirely different perspective on life. I knew that if the treatment didn't work, I would be in heaven soon. I also knew that every day I was alive was an opportunity to share Jesus.

Hebrews 12:2 portrays Jesus' outlook on His own death sentence; *"For the joy set before him he endured the cross, scorning its shame."*(NIV) As Christians, when we face death, we too can count it all joy, knowing that because of Jesus, we have life beyond the grave.

*"Brothers and sisters, I do not consider myself
yet to have taken hold of it. But one thing I
do: Forgetting what is behind and straining
toward what is ahead, I press on toward
the goal to win the prize for which God has
called me heavenward in Christ Jesus."*

Phillipians 3:13-14 (NIV)

PARALYZING PAST

In Zechariah 7:4-7, God is rebuking the returned exiles for fasting in memory of the sinfulness that led them to Babylon. God asks them *"When you fasted and mourned in the fifth and seventh months during those seventy years, <u>did you really fast for Me; for Me?</u> ... <u>Should you not have obeyed </u>the words which the Lord proclaimed through the former..."* (NKJV Emphasis added) Obedience is what God wants, yet these Jews had made a ritual of fasting in memory of several disasters, including the capture of Jerusalem and the destruction of the Temple. These tragedies were God's judgement, and a result of their sin.

God doesn't want us dwelling on our past sins or the consequences of them. He wants us actively seeking Him.

F.B. Meyer states that, *"There is no need to observe the sad*

anniversaries of our sins and their accompanying punishment, …..
When He forgives and restores, the need for dwelling on the bitter
past is over…Too many of us are always dwelling beside the graves
of the dead past." (Our Daily Homily, Volume 13, p.86)

Sometimes, as Christians, we let our past mistakes cling to us like a badge. Maybe we asked God's forgiveness, but then weeks or months later are reminded of what we did. It could be that the repercussions of our sin nag us and the consequences of our sin make us feel like we weren't forgiven.

But God's forgiveness is permanent. He doesn't bring up our sin once it's covered by the blood of Christ. Satan may remind us, we may remind ourselves, and consequences may bring them to mind. However, consequences are not an indication of unforgiven sin; they are only the result of sin. God never promised that His forgiveness would eliminate the repercussions of sin, only the eternal punishment.

When we dwell on our failures or the results of them, we cripple our efforts to please God. Are you allowing your past sin to paralyze your walk with God? If so, read 1 John 1:9 and believe.

> *"They had called for the apostles and beaten them, … and let them go. So they departed from the presence of the council, rejoicing that they were counted worthy to suffer shame for His name."*
>
> Acts 5:40-41 (NKJV)

PRECIOUS PERSECUTION

A number of years ago, during a church service in Europe, a group of soldiers stormed into the sanctuary. With rigid expressions and guns in hand, they demanded, "Anyone willing to deny Jesus Christ may leave now." The majority of parishioners scurried to freedom. To the few who remained, the band of armed men relaxed their demeanor. They set down their weapons and remarked, "Now we know who the real Christians are."

Would you deny Christ to save your life? At first consideration, we'd all like to think we would not. How about denying Christ to save your spouse's life? Your child's life? The prospect is disconcerting. Suddenly, it's not so easy to answer. In fact, at this point, many would begin to rationalize how they could deny Christ outwardly, but inwardly remain faithful.

Foxe's Book of Martyrs tells the 3rd century account of a young boy, who, when called out of a multitude of Christians, professed that Christ was the true God. When the prefect heard this testimony, he ordered that the boy be scourged, while his mother stood by. She encouraged him all the while. The next day he was taken from prison and led to his execution where his mother said, "Farewell, my sweet child; and when thou hast entered the kingdom of Christ, there in thy blest estate remember thy mother."

If this is hard to imagine, it's because we have long lived in comfort and freedom. Without the fear of being punished for Christ's sake, we have become complacent. Yet, persecution is still rampant in many countries and thousands of Christians worldwide are martyred for their faith.

Jesus' return is imminent, yet, it's very possible we will face severe persecution in this country before He comes. We are already seeing a vicious intolerance toward those who take a stand against immoral laws.

It's time we prepare for the worse by deepening our relationship with Jesus Christ. Then, if persecution comes, we can rejoice in suffering for His Name! Because as Peter said, *"Rejoice inasmuch as you participate in the sufferings of Christ."* (1 Peter 4:13 NIV)

*"Now faith is confidence in what we hope for
and assurance about what we do not see."*

Hebrews 11:1 (NIV)

FAITH 101

When Rut and her husband Kemy had adopted their first son from China, they were amazed at how God worked out so many details. Time and again, their heavenly Father provided for their needs.

Having seen such power in God's provision, they felt called to adopt a second child. This new journey began only six months after Sammy came to live with them, prompting some cautionary advice from loved ones. The warnings intensified when Rut shared the news that their next child was diagnosed with brain damage and congenital heart disease.

Having talked with a few doctors about the medical issues, they were given an uncertain prognosis. Yet, God spoke to them through His Word. James 1:27 resonated in their hearts: *"Religion that God our Father accepts as pure and faultless is this: to look after orphans and widows in their distress and to keep oneself from being polluted by the world."* (NIV)

With peace in their hearts, they moved ahead with the

adoption, trusting in God's faithfulness. Throughout the process, they prayed for the little boy they had never met, knowing that soon, he would be their son.

Finally, they made their trip to Asia and brought little Diel home. During those first weeks, Rut and Kemy praised God for the sweet bonding that took place in their family. Additionally, they took Diel to see specialists, including a neurologist and a cardiologist. By the grace of God, these doctors pronounced their son perfectly healthy. Whether God healed him or whether he had been misdiagnosed is uncertain. But Rut and Kemy do know that God wanted them to trust Him completely, and that is what they did.

Before Diel came home, Rut and Kemy were not sure how a severe special-needs child would impact their lives. Yet they believed God created him for a higher purpose and knew that the Lord would equip them as his parents.

Looking back, Rut can't help but give all the glory to God, for He is a *"Father to the fatherless,"* (Psalm 68:5 NIV) and *"He cares for the orphans,"* (Psalm 146:9 NIV). She learned that when God calls you to do something, it's best to trust Him with all your heart. He'll take care of the rest!

"From one man he made all the nations,
that they should inhabit the whole earth;
and he marked out their appointed times in
history and the boundaries of their lands.
God did this so that they would seek him
and perhaps reach out for him and find him,
though he is not far from any one of us."

Acts 17:26-27 (NIV)

SEEK AND FIND

I played a game as a child where, blindfolded, one would try to guess an object by handling it. The toy, utensil, or trinket had to be identified by its shape, texture, and size. For the challenger, the trick was to find something so obscure that the player would not be able to visualize it.

I remember one difficult object that I had discerned was molded plastic with an odd shape, but remained a mystery. Refusing to give in, I earnestly thought about the piece, hoping to connect it with something familiar. Then awareness dawned. I pictured my brother's plastic army men set. The object was a battleground accessory - a little rock wall.

In Acts 17, Paul told those in Athens about the God of

Creation, who created man and blessed man on the earth so man might seek after Him in return. Paul explained that as man sees creation, he should reach out for the Creator and find Him.

To "reach out" means to "grope", as a blind person would do in order to find their way. When a person blinded by sin, accepts that there is a Creator, all he needs to do is reach out to that Creator. By reaching out, that one will find Him - in the sense of *getting to know* God. The verse ends with the promise that God is not far.

To the world, creation itself is enough to convince people there is God, but all too often, they refuse to accept that He exists. Yet for those who make the choice to reach out, like in the game mentioned, they can discern who God is and find Him.

Like a blind person feeling his way along a path, seekers who earnestly search, will find the truth. *"You will seek me and find me when you seek me with all your heart."* (Jeremiah 29:13 NIV)

Eventually, the truth will become evident, like removing the blindfold and recognizing everything.

*"Do everything without grumbling or
arguing, so that you may become blameless
and pure, "children of God without fault
in a warped and crooked generation." Then
you will shine among them like stars in the
sky as you hold firmly to the word of life."*

Philippians 2:14-16 (NIV)

SHINE ON

"Society is spiraling out of control!" my friend uttered, bemoaning the current headlines. She rambled on distressfully, referencing the news. "This world is so dark!" was her final reply.

We'd been enjoying the beautiful day sipping iced coffee on the patio of a favorite café. But when our conversation turned to her complaint, the lighthearted mood began to fade. I looked up at the sky, "How many stars do you see?"

Tilting her head back, she furrowed her brow, "There aren't any stars out." I disagreed, "Of course there are."

"Well, yeah, they're up there, but we can't see them," she clarified, "It's too light out." "Exactly!"

As the forces of evil overshadow this world, God's Word

calls us to be lights. Just as the stars are more brilliant on the darkest nights, our lives shine brighter in this dark world.

As a photographer, I often utilize the quality of black velvet to shoot pictures of small objects. When a client asked me to shoot her handcrafted jewelry, the smooth fabric was the perfect backdrop.

Because velvet absorbs light, it remains very dark, even under bright lights. The color and sparkle of each pedant shimmered in contrast to the background. When I intensified the lights to illuminate the shot, the gems became more brilliant, because the velvet absorbed, not reflected the light.

Like gems on a velvet backdrop, our lives stand out in this world, because the light of Christ is shining down on us. However, if we "tarnish" ourselves with a grumbling spirit and a compromising walk, we lose our brilliance.

Jesus, our Light Source, says to us, *"Let your light shine before others, that they may see your good deeds and glorify your Father in heaven."* (Matthew 5:16 NIV) We are called to be lights in this world.

As we glisten with joy, sparkle with peace and radiate the love of Christ, we bring honor and glory to the One Who lives in us. Let us stay polished and pure. Let's **shine on** for Jesus!

Printed in the United States
By Bookmasters